100 MORE THINGS
YOU DON'T NEED A MAN FOR!

Exterior Home and Yard Maintenance

100 MORE THINGS

YOU DON'T NEED A MAN FOR!

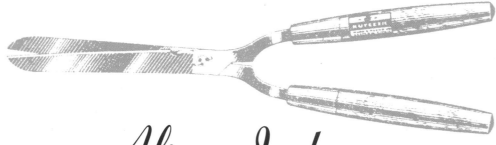

Alison Jenkins

LAUREL
GLEN

San Diego, California

LAUREL GLEN PUBLISHING

An imprint of the Advantage Publishers Group

5880 Oberlin Drive, San Diego, CA 92121-4794

www.advantagebooksonline.com

This book was conceived, designed, and produced by

THE IVY PRESS LIMITED

The Old Candlemakers, West Street

Lewes, East Sussex BN7 2NZ, England

Creative Director: PETER BRIDGEWATER

Publisher: SOPHIE COLLINS

Editorial Director: STEVE LUCK

Art Director: CLARE BARBER

Designer: KEVIN KNIGHT

Mac Design: GINNY ZEAL

Senior Project Editor: CAROLINE EARLE

Photographer: CALVEY TAYLOR-HAW

Additional Photography: PAUL MANSER

Illustrators: ANNA HUNTER-DOWNING, IVAN HISSEY

Picture Researcher: SHARON DORTENZIO

ISBN 1-57145-825-5

Library of Congress Cataloging-in-Publication Data available on request.

Printed and bound by Hong Kong Graphics and Printing, China

1 2 3 4 5 06 05 04 03 02

Contents

ANOTHER
100
MAN-FREE
ACTIVITIES!

✳ WHY DON'T
WE DO IT IN
THE YARD?

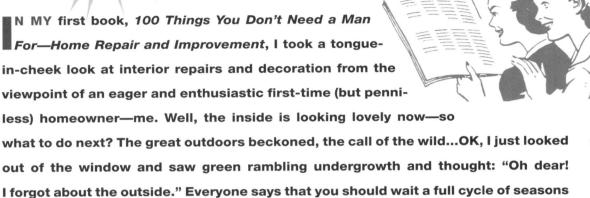

TIME TO GET YOUR TOOLS OUT AGAIN!

Introduction

IN MY first book, *100 Things You Don't Need a Man For—Home Repair and Improvement*, I took a tongue-in-cheek look at interior repairs and decoration from the viewpoint of an eager and enthusiastic first-time (but penniless) homeowner—me. Well, the inside is looking lovely now—so what to do next? The great outdoors beckoned, the call of the wild...OK, I just looked out of the window and saw green rambling undergrowth and thought: "Oh dear! I forgot about the outside." Everyone says that you should wait a full cycle of seasons before doing anything to the garden so you know what's there, bulbs and stuff like that—but I don't think that applies to mowing the grass!

I don't really intend to talk about gardening here, what I'm talking about is simple repairs and maintenance from the rooftop to the drains, exterior decorating and fencing, patios and pathways, outdoor living, decks, and diggin' dirt, with a bit of garden taming thrown in for good measure! So let's talk about the exterior—the yard, the garden, call it what you will, your outside space is an extension of the inside and is deserving of as much attention. Your garden should be a space for relaxing and entertaining, for being at one with nature or barbecuing with your friends! That brings us to the question: "Why do it yourself?" Well, ladies, if, like me, you have big ideas and a small bank balance, then the answer is crystal clear—cash! I like to have fun and I also like to shop, so if I can save myself some money on the home improvement front then I will quite happily do so—more money to spend on shoes! Why spend all your hard-earned cash on hired help if you can do it yourself?

HEY, LOOK, MORE HOME IMPROVEMENT, GIRLS—AND THIS TIME WE GET TO PLAY WITH CHAINSAWS!

LET ME AT THAT HEAVY MACHINERY!

MY, LOOK AT THAT LOVELY WHEELBARROW!

I'VE BEEN SO WORRIED SINCE SHE ASKED FOR A BULLDOZER FOR OUR ANNIVERSARY!

Most basic maintenance or repair tasks are simple; you just need to know how and what to do. This book will tell it like it is, plain and simple—no complicated jargon that'll have your eyes glazed over in a minute, and hopefully, you'll have a giggle, too. But girls, don't forget, the joy of home improvement is knowing how, what, and when to do it. It's also about knowing when not to—check out the last section when you find yourself requiring the services of a man who can.

When embarking upon an outdoor home-improvement task, basic principles apply, so don't forget the two *P*s—Preparation Pays! If a job's worth doing, then it is worth doing well; thorough preparation is essential to achieving successful results. Accessories, too, are vital, as every girl knows. Take this opportunity to add to your toolbox (or start one if you haven't got one!), and remember to choose the right tool for the job—matching accessories! Browse at your leisure through the "Tools Out!" section. Make sure you have all the right stuff to make your home improvement tasks a cinch.

So girls, with the aid of this book you'll be fully tooled up, outfitted, and ready to go in no time. Anyone know what color rubber boots we'll be wearing next season? Enjoy!

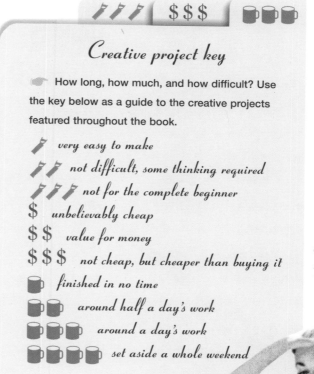

Creative project key

How long, how much, and how difficult? Use the key below as a guide to the creative projects featured throughout the book.

🪚 *very easy to make*

🪚🪚 *not difficult, some thinking required*

🪚🪚🪚 *not for the complete beginner*

$ *unbelievably cheap*

$ $ *value for money*

$ $ $ *not cheap, but cheaper than buying it*

☕ *finished in no time*

☕☕ *around half a day's work*

☕☕☕ *around a day's work*

☕☕☕☕ *set aside a whole weekend*

✳ HMM...I'M ALWAYS ON THE LOOKOUT FOR AN OUTDOOR PROJECT...

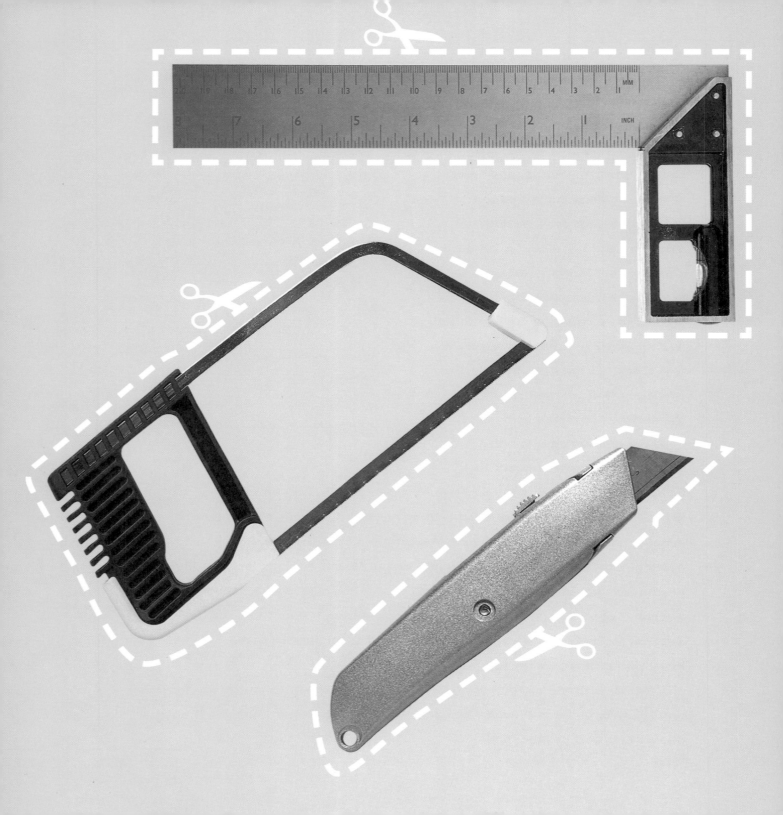

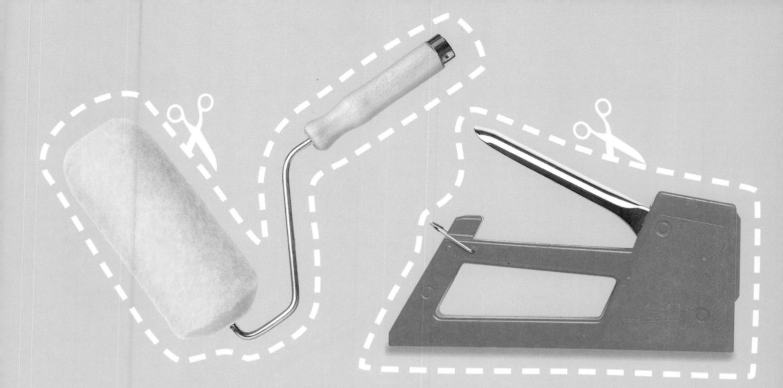

TOOLS OUT!

Here we have lots of wonderful tools for outdoor maintenance. What a shopping opportunity!

Tooling up for the great outdoors

Most indoor home improvement tools contained in a girl's basic toolbox can be put to equally good use outdoors, too. If you have already got your basic kit together, give yourself a pat on the back and read on smugly! However, if the words "tool kit" have an unfamiliar ring, don't despair, just peruse the following pages of tools and materials—some essential, some nonessential, and some to rent for that one-time-only job. Remember: you don't have to rush to the hardware store and get everything at once; just buy a few essentials first and then add to your collection as and when required.

HAND TOOLS BASIC

"But all tools are hand tools because you use your hands," I can hear you say. That's true, but what I'm talking about are "hand" as opposed to "power" tools. That is, tools that don't run on electricity from either an outlet or a battery. You have to use your own elbow grease to work them—the power tools will come later on. These versatile hand tools are just as useful outdoors as they are indoors.

Staple gun

Use this to attach lightweight materials in place, for example fly screening or canvas.

No unpleasant grinding with this—when the blade's blunt, just chuck it!

Hacksaw

There are general-purpose and mini hacksaws. Both types cut metal tubes, rods, and sheets. Use the big hacksaw for larger jobs and the smaller one to cut in constricted areas.

Screwdrivers

You can get a matching set of screwdrivers in any hardware store. You will find flat-head screwdrivers for use with screws with a slotted head, and Phillips screwdrivers for screws with a cross-shaped indentation in the head.

Pliers

A set of three: long-nose, slip-joint, and a snippy one called a side-cutter. To grip, bend, squeeze, or shape wires or metal.

Utility knife

Everyone should have a utility knife, preferably one with a retractable blade so that it is safe in the tool bag. Use it for general lightweight cutting and scoring, but be careful not to cut yourself.

Locking pliers

This combination holds things together while you work. Use the adjusting screw to vary the width of the jaws, then squeeze the pliers shut. Press the release lever to loosen wrench.

Chalk line

Use this little gadget to make a straight line to guide you in getting things lined up.

CAN'T DO WITHOUT

Tenon saw Use this rigid saw for making straight cuts across wood.

Chisel set A set of three (small, medium, and large) will suffice. Used in woodwork for paring, trimming, and cutting out waste.

Claw hammer This heavy, versatile, general-purpose hammer is a tool kit "must have." The "claw" at the back of the hammer head is used to lever out nails.

Cross-peen hammer A lightweight tool used to drive in small nails, brads, and tacks.

Center punch This hard metal punch marks the center of holes to be drilled, in materials such as metal.

Straightedge Keep a long, sturdy metal ruler handy for drawing straight lines or for when you are using a utility knife to cut something.

Awl This is a small hand tool with a pointed spike, useful for making pilot holes in wood before driving in a screw; good for making holes in other materials, too.

More indoor tools for outdoor uses

POWER TOOLS

Now we're talking! Power tools can be the plug-into-the-outlet type or the cordless variety that runs on an internal rechargeable battery. Either way, power tools are fabulous pieces of equipment and will make your home improvement tasks easier.

Electric drill

A drill was my very first power-tool purchase and is an absolute essential in my opinion—with a cord or without. Make sure it has variable speeds and a hammer function as an option.

Drill bits

Start with a set of multi-purpose drill bits—for both wood and masonry—then add to the collection. You should also get a few flat or spade bits, for making larger holes, and a countersink bit, which makes a nice recess so that the screwhead lies flush.

Electric screwdriver

Yet another of those "must haves." A power screwdriver really is the ticket if you've got lots of screws to drive in—or out, because you can unscrew with it, too. Saves getting nasty blisters on your hands.

USING ELECTRICITY OUTDOORS SAFELY

☞ When using electrically powered equipment, take the necessary safety precautions, especially when working outdoors. Substitute GFCI (Ground Fault Circuit Interrupter) breakers for standard receptacles, especially in kitchens, bathrooms, garages, workshops, and outdoor areas. These automatically "trip" and cut off the electricity supply to protect you from electric shock (for instance, if you mow over your lawnmower cord by mistake). There are several types of GFCIs. Portable GFCIs plug into a three-slot receptacle and will protect individual wall outlets. A wall receptacle GFCI is installed in an outlet in place of a standard receptacle. A circuit breaker GFCI is fitted at the service panel to protect selected circuits. Consult a qualified electrician about installing GFCIs. A GFCI should be used whenever you are using power tools. Cordless tools are probably the ideal solution in an outdoor situation.

* OH, NO, SOMEONE'S TAKEN THE KITCHEN SINK!

Jigsaw

Believe me, a jigsaw is a truly wonderful thing—essential for cutting curves and wiggly lines, but also useful for making fast, straight cuts. Most jigsaws will have an adjustable guide for this purpose, so that you will be able to cut parallel to an edge, for example.

WARNING

☞ Power tools can be dangerous if not used properly and with care. Always read the operating manual before use and make sure that you understand all the instructions.

☞ Always switch off the power supply when changing bits or blades, and make sure these are securely fitted before you start work.

☞ Don't use a power tool with a worn or frayed cord.

☞ Tie your hair back and don't wear very loose clothing while using power tools, to keep anything from getting caught.

Portable workbench

This is not essential, but is extremely useful when working outdoors—a nice portable work surface for sawing on and so on.

Power sander

This is definitely one of those "can't do without" labor-saving devices. Sanding is laborious and time-consuming, but it is very important to do it properly and thoroughly if you want good results. Anything that saves time and effort gets my vote, so invest in a belt or orbital sander, as well as a detail sander for awkward corners.

Outdoor extension cord

Unless you are fully tooled up with cordless items, you will need an extension cord in order to use your power tools outside. Get a long, heavy-duty, exterior one. Do NOT use one meant for indoor use—this could be dangerous.

AIN'T NOTHING LIKE THE REEL THING, BABY!

What type of tool for the roof?

ROOFING AND SIDING

GOING UP!

"Help!" I hear you cry, "this is a job for the big boys." Don't panic, I'm not talking major roof installation here, just a little repair and maintenance here and there. Any girl worth the name can patch up cracked tiles that are within easy reach. Carrying out minor repairs to roofs and siding will save you money in the long run—and it's well worth investing in some of these useful tools.

Tin snips
Essential when up on the roof. Try cutting metal, vinyl material, or flashing with anything else, and you'll have problems. Remember: always get the right tool for the job.

Plugging chisel
Use one of these to remove all the old, loose mortar joints when you have a repointing job to do. Place the point in the mortar, then tap the head with a sledgehammer.

✻ BOY, DOES YOUR ROOF NEED SOME NEW TILES!

Sliding bevel
A gadget that helps you to measure angles accurately so that you can cut your materials to fit neatly.

Angled putty knife
Use this handy tool for applying and shaping filler.

TOOLS TO RENT

Power circular saw You may need one of these for cutting siding and other materials. It is also possible to cut masonry materials with it, but you'll need a diamond blade for this. Best to rent one, because you'll probably only need to use it once in a while.

Goggles and mask

Wear these when handling or cutting abrasive materials. They don't look very gorgeous, but better safe than sorry.

MORE

ESSENTIALS

Ladder You'll never get up on the roof without one of these. See pages 18–19 for further information.

Chalk line This gadget will make a straight line to guide you in getting things lined up (*see also page 11*).

Steel tape You need this for measuring— especially for measuring long distances.

Screwdrivers Borrow these from your general toolbox to help you get those screws in and out.

Caulking gun Handy if you have a lot of caulking to do. You can use a putty knife and filling compound, but it'll take longer and be more messy.

Claw hammer To pry out all the old nails and bang in those nice new ones.

Prybar/crowbar This helps you to lever out nails and to lift boards and panels.

Utility knife Keep this old favorite on hand if you need to do some lightweight cutting or trimming.

Slate ripper A specialized tool used for cutting and ripping out old roofing nails when replacing roof tiles.

Use a bench plane to keep wood smooth and trim.

Try square

Used as a guide when marking out siding boards or other materials. Ensures your cut will be perfectly straight and corners truly square.

Plumb line

Handy when you need to mark a true vertical.

Bench plane

This is ideal for trimming end grain and beveling edges.

What types of tools for patios and paths?

BRICKS AND MORTAR

LAY LADY LAY

Bricklaying takes years of practice to perfect. I don't suggest that you attempt a huge building project, but with patience, you can certainly manage to rebuild a low garden wall, create a raised flowerbed, and even tackle a small repointing job. Patios and paths are also manageable projects. Here are some of the tools that you may need, should you have an urge in the bricks-and-mortar department.

Rubber mallet

My favorite! When you're laying your patio, you'll need to gently whack the slabs with this to make sure they have set nice and level.

Pointing trowel

A pointed hand tool for shaping the mortar joints between courses of bricks.

Short-handled sledgehammer

Use this with a brick chisel to cut a brick or stone in half or to size.

Carpenter's pencil

This fat pencil is the only thing to use when marking out bricks or stones—an ordinary pencil point would simply snap in half.

TOOLS TO RENT

Concrete mixer You can rent one of these for mixing concrete in large quantities. You can either get a great big one or a little cute one, so that you can mix smaller "large" quantities—if you see what I mean.

Plate vibrator This is an electrically powered flattening machine. Use it when you've laid your patio or path to make sure that all the bricks or slabs are firmly embedded.

Guillotine cutter This is a hydraulic device for cutting pavers. It is an absolute "must" if you have to cut a lot of slabs into awkward shapes.

Steel tape

Keep your steel tape measure handy for all your measuring needs.

Brick chisel

This is available in different sizes; the wide blade is perfect for cutting bricks, blocks, and paving slabs.

Cold chisel

Use this with a hammer for cutting paving slabs, metal, and so on.

Mason's line and pins

A nylon line strung between two pegs. Use these to mark a straight line for setting out the courses of paving stones, bricks, and so on.

Gloves

Those gloves again! Not especially attractive, but if it's them or your fingernails, then I'd choose the gloves every time.

CAN'T DO WITHOUT

Sledgehammer A big, heavy brute, useful for driving in a cold chisel or brick chisel and for general heavy bashing.

Raking tool/plugging chisel Use one of these to remove all the old loose mortar joints when you have a repointing job to do. Place the point in the mortar, then tap the head with a sledgehammer (*see also page 15*).

Brick trowel This is a fatter sibling of the pointing trowel, used to scoop up and position mortar when laying bricks.

Jointer This is a hand tool with a narrow, rounded blade, used for smoothing out and shaping the mortar joints between brickwork courses, or when pointing.

Try square For accurate marking out.

Crowbar For general prying and levering.

Stiff broom For sweeping up all the mess you've made and for brushing a dry mix into the cracks of paving materials.

Frenchman This is a little hand tool used for scooping up excess mortar from joints. You can make one by heating the end of an ordinary knife, then bending it at right angles (*see page 71*).

Goggles and mask Wear these when handling or cutting abrasive materials.

Level

An absolutely essential tool. If you're laying bricks or paving, you really need to make sure that everything is completely level—both horizontally and vertically.

Getting High

ALL ABOUT LADDERS AND ACCESS EQUIPMENT

Get on up there! Sooner or later you will need a ladder of some sort. A lightweight, aluminum, five- or seven-rung, folding stepladder is sufficient for indoor use. However, the great outdoors is another matter—unless, of course, you live in a very short house. Providing adequate access to the work area is very important indeed, and it really isn't worth compromising your safety by not getting the proper equipment. Teetering and tottering on a makeshift arrangement will only end in tears.

RENTAL OPTIONS

☞ Ask the rental store staff to show you how to use this equipment safely.

Scaffold tower Here, sectional frames are joined together to make an access tower. You can build it to the height you need.

Trestles and staging You can rent these to construct a safe and stable work platform to suit your needs.

Work platform This is a little platform unit with lockable wheels on each leg. Put it where you want it, secure it, and up you go.

Dual-purpose ladder

This very clever device converts from a stepladder to a straight ladder. A handy compromise between an ordinary stepladder and an extension ladder.

* WHAT'S WITH THE FLYING GOGGLES? WE LIVE IN A BUNGALOW!

ONE DAY, SON, YOU'LL BE AS TALL AS I AM.

LADDER LESSONS

Raising a ladder Lay the ladder on the ground with the feet against the wall. Raise it slowly to a vertical position while walking toward the wall. Gradually pull the feet away from the wall to a suitable position.

Using a ladder stay It may be the stuff of slapstick movies, but you don't want the feet of the ladder to slip and for you and it to take a dive, so always secure them to the ground using a ladder stay. On soft or uneven ground, place the feet on a piece of board with a wooden cleat screwed along one edge. This will prevent the feet of the ladder from sinking or slipping away. Then sink two pegs into the ground next to the cleat edge to secure it. Next, tie a piece of rope around the feet and secure it to another peg sunk firmly into the ground between the feet and the wall. You can buy stabilizers like little metal legs that bolt onto the ladder if the ground is too hard to sink pegs into.

Accessories

Get yourself some accessories to make life aloft more comfortable. A tool tray is a good idea; it clips onto the top of the ladder and holds your tools within easy reach. A paint-bucket hook to hang your paint bucket from is also useful—with one of these you'll always have one hand free with which to hang onto the ladder.

Extension ladder

Double or triple extension ladders are used to get really high. Some are operated by a rope-and-pulley system, so that you can easily extend them yourself.

✳ SO IT'S ONE SMALL STEP FOR A WOMAN, ONE GIANT STEP FOR WOMANKIND!

TIP

Never leave ladders unattended outside your home. Always lock them up securely or store them in a garage or shed, if you have one. An untrustworthy character may take advantage of such an opportunity to break into your home and make off with your valuables.

SAFETY

☞ Do NOT be tempted to save a journey up and down by stretching sideways to reach the next bit of work. A stretch too far and you're off the ladder plummeting earthward.

☞ Never climb higher than four rungs from the top—you'll lose your balance and fall.

☞ Position the foot of a ladder about 3 ft. out from the wall for every 12 ft. of the ladder's extended length. A ladder should be leaned at a safe angle—usually around 70°.

☞ When using an extension ladder, make sure the extended sections overlap by at least one quarter of their length.

☞ Always check a ladder before using it. Make sure there is no rotten wood and that the hardware and hinges are in good repair.

Rope

An essential accessory for a ladder stay (*see box opposite*).

Here come the big boys

SERIOUS TOOLS FOR RENT

YEAH BABE

Okay, I know that I'm always stressing the importance of building up a wonderful tool kit, but some things you really do not need to buy. It may be tempting, but resist! Look in the phone book and get the number of your local rental store—they will have everything you could possibly need for rent at daily rates or, even better, weekend rates. The staff are usually very helpful and will tell you all you need to know about how these gadgets work. They will supply all the accessories and safety equipment, too.

AND HERE'S MORE...

Guillotine cutter This is the only machine to use if you have lots of stones or pavers to cut—a real time and effort saver.

Access equipment If you need a really long ladder or an access platform, trestles, or a tower, rent one to suit your needs.

Earth tamper Basically a heavy, flat plate on a stick, used for flattening/tamping down earth. Simply hold the handle firmly with both hands, then bash the plate onto the ground.

Angle grinder Electrically powered tool with a heavy-duty revolving blade, used for cutting and shaping brick, stone, or metal.

Drain augers

This set comprises a long, flexible coiled wire with a crank-handle at one end. You can rent drain auger attachments, including a plunger head, a corkscrew head, and a scraper head.

Posthole auger

A tool for making holes for fence posts. If you have a lot of fence posts to set, this will be very useful indeed.

Chainsaw

Use one of these to cut up large logs, or even to cut down an unwanted tree (*see safety box on page 22*).

* OKAY, SO I FEEL REALLY SILLY...CAN I COME OUT NOW...PLEASE?

Water pump

If you are unfortunate enough to have a flood in your basement, then you will need one of these to tackle the problem. You can also rent huge hot-air blowers for drying out damp areas.

Concrete mixer

When you have to mix large quantities of concrete, you need to use one of these. They are available in various sizes, and the store staff will advise you on the correct size for the job.

THE ONLY VIBRATOR THAT YOU CAN PLUG INTO AN OUTLET!

Circular saw

This is well worth considering if you intend to cut a lot of heavy lumber or large sheet materials.

Plate vibrator

Once you've laid your patio, use this vibrating machine to ensure that all your slabs or bricks are level and properly embedded.

More heavyweights

TOOLS TO TRY THEN BUY

SCARY BUT GOOD!

Say you've rented a piece of heavy-duty equipment just to give it a try, but then find you can't live without it. Go ahead and make that purchase. Some pieces of equipment, such as the power washer, are so much fun to use that you will never want to use elbow grease again!

Edger

This is handy for trimming straggly bits of grass along the edges or around trees. But don't think you can do a whole lawn with this— it's solely for trimming.

SAFETY

☞ Your own personal safety and that of others is of the utmost importance when using power tools outdoors. Always wear the protective clothing provided by the rental store. Also, warn neighbors if you're using noisy equipment—if you're wearing ear protectors you may not notice a child, pet, or person passing by. Better safe than sorry. Test GFCIs before using an outdoor extension cord with electrically powered tools and equipment.

Hard hat and ear protectors

Wear these to protect yourself from something falling on your head, or when using noisy equipment.

JUST THE THING FOR REALLY BAD HAIR DAYS!

Power saw

This fantastic machine takes the sweat out of sawing. It's hard work being up a ladder, trying to saw off branches. Use the power saw! It can cut pipes, lumber, and all sorts of other things, too.

Hedge trimmer

If you have an untidy hedge or bush, trim it into a neat shape in no time with this.

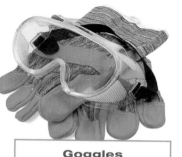

Goggles and gloves

Handling scary equipment with sharp blades calls for more heavy-duty goggles and gloves.

* SEE HERE, MISTER, I'M GONNA CLEAN UP THIS TOWN WHETHER YOU LIKE IT OR NOT!

ACCESSORIES

Specialized blades and bits

You probably already have a basic set of accessories for your power tools, but if you need a really large masonry bit, a diamond blade for cutting masonry with the circular saw, or a long jigsaw blade, then the tool rental store will again come to your aid. Just ask them for what you need, and they will undoubtedly come up with the goods—for a small fee, of course. Never attempt to perform a heavy-duty task with an ordinary bit or blade.

Power washer

What was I saying about not needing to buy everything? These are so good that you may want one of your own. Use it to clean the car, patio, windows, walls, fences, siding...

Garden shredder

This nifty little garden item is very popular for shredding twigs, leaves, and other organic debris.

Tools that come in handy for all kinds of outdoor tasks

ODDBALL TOOLS FOR SPECIFIC JOBS

I love oddball tools and have quite a few tucked away in my toolbox as we speak, just waiting for that special task to present itself! "Be prepared"—that's my motto. Have a look at this selection—perhaps something will appeal to you. Remember: it pays to get the right tool for the job.

Hex keys

These come in a set and are useful for tightening up setscrews. But make sure that you get the right size for the right screw. They're also indispensable for anything that comes in kit form.

Pipe cutter

A handy gadget that is available in various sizes and specially designed for cutting metal pipes of different diameters.

Clamshell posthole digger

If you intend to do lots of fencing, and need to dig lots of holes, then one of these will probably be a very good purchase. And you can use it for digging holes in general, holes for plants, and so on.

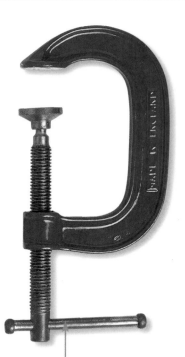

C-clamp

Useful tools for holding things in position while you saw, glue, and so on.

Large cultivator

This has a claw-shaped arrangement of prongs. Place the prongs in the earth, then wiggle the handle to break up the surface of the earth.

Lopper

Like giant pruners with long handles, they're very useful when tackling unruly trees and undergrowth. It lops off those branches with ease.

ODDS AND ENDS

Blowtorch Use this for removing very thick paint and for heating up metal pipes for bending.

Miter saw I think this is a very useful item to own. I have to admit I don't use it that often, but when I do, I think, "What a fab tool this is!" It enables you to make angled cuts in wood, especially molding, and is essential for making picture frames.

Small cultivator

This is the baby to the daddy on the left. Suitable for use in small areas; just place the prongs in the earth, then wiggle it clockwise and counter-clockwise to break up the earth.

Pickax

I suspect you will get similar pleasure from wielding a pickax, though this tool is more for breaking things up than for demolition—for example, breaking up an old concrete path or paving stones. You can then use the pointed head like a lever to lift and remove the broken pieces.

Sledgehammer

A long-handled sledgehammer doesn't fool around. Whenever you need to demolish something, such as a stud partition wall, this is the only way to do it. Wield it with caution, though, as you don't want to demolish more than you bargained for. After a few hefty thwacks you will be a sledgehammer convert.

❋ YOU'VE SIMPLY GOT TO HAVE THE RIGHT TOOLS FOR THE JOB!

Making the earth move

LANDSCAPING TOOLS DIG IT

Are you happy with your landscape? If not, then you may well like to change it—perhaps making it flat where there are bumps or introducing some contours where there is flatness. And if your great outdoors resembles a jungle, then you need some serious defoliation gear. That's the problem with living things such as trees, grass, and plants—left to their own devices they just GROW! You have to show them who's boss before it's too late.

* YOU DON'T REALLY NEED A MAN TO CUT THE LAWN, DO YOU?

Pruners
A heavy-duty hand snipper for pruning branches and general trimming. Don't try to cut branches or twigs with ordinary household scissors—it will ruin them.

I LIKE TO THINK I'M ON THE CUTTING EDGE!

Pruning/folding knife
This takes the hard work out of cutting thick twigs or branches—then just folds away afterward.

Shears
Like a giant pair of scissors with big handles for general trimming and for tidying undergrowth, such as hedges or bushes. Don't cut thick twigs or branches with these—use a pruner.

Mower
There are numerous types, from basic models like this and ones with grass catchers and scarifiers, to mini tractor versions. You can tame most lawns with a small-to-average-sized mower.

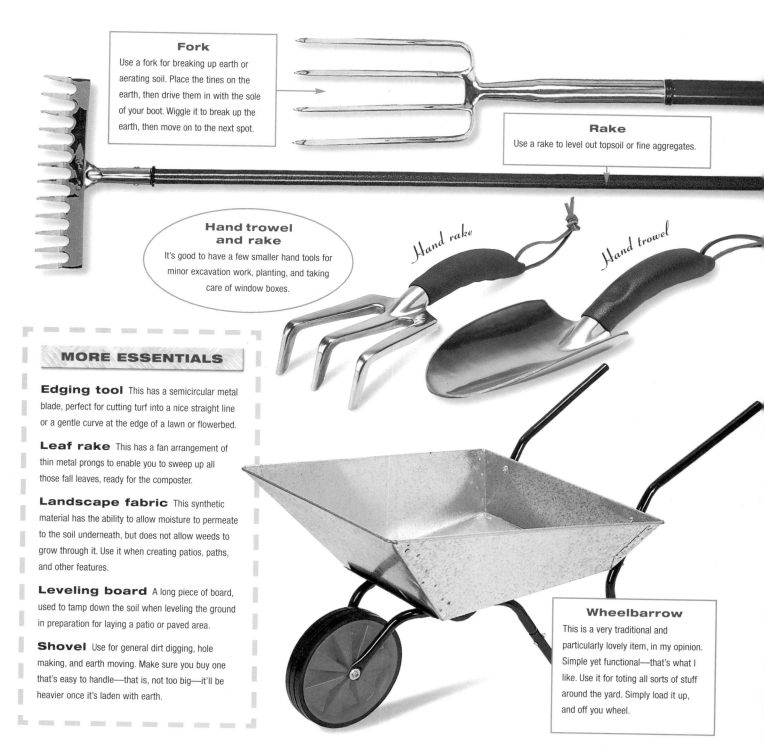

Fork

Use a fork for breaking up earth or aerating soil. Place the tines on the earth, then drive them in with the sole of your boot. Wiggle it to break up the earth, then move on to the next spot.

Rake

Use a rake to level out topsoil or fine aggregates.

Hand trowel and rake

It's good to have a few smaller hand tools for minor excavation work, planting, and taking care of window boxes.

Hand rake

Hand trowel

MORE ESSENTIALS

Edging tool This has a semicircular metal blade, perfect for cutting turf into a nice straight line or a gentle curve at the edge of a lawn or flowerbed.

Leaf rake This has a fan arrangement of thin metal prongs to enable you to sweep up all those fall leaves, ready for the composter.

Landscape fabric This synthetic material has the ability to allow moisture to permeate to the soil underneath, but does not allow weeds to grow through it. Use it when creating patios, paths, and other features.

Leveling board A long piece of board, used to tamp down the soil when leveling the ground in preparation for laying a patio or paved area.

Shovel Use for general dirt digging, hole making, and earth moving. Make sure you buy one that's easy to handle—that is, not too big—it'll be heavier once it's laden with earth.

Wheelbarrow

This is a very traditional and particularly lovely item, in my opinion. Simple yet functional—that's what I like. Use it for toting all sorts of stuff around the yard. Simply load it up, and off you wheel.

Time to get the brushes out!

EXTERIOR DECORATING TOOLS AND EQUIPMENT

A brush is a brush is a brush…. Not so, my friend, for there are numerous brushes (and rollers) to suit all sorts of painting and decorating jobs. I've concentrated here on exterior decorating. You'll see some masonry brushes (the big ones) and a few for woodwork; the other items just make life easier for you.

✳ ALL THESE BRUSHES AND I STILL CAN'T DO A THING WITH MY HAIR!

Drop cloths

Spread drop cloths over areas you don't want to paint, such as the doorstep and patio. This saves you the hassle of cleaning up drips and splashes afterward.

Woodwork paintbrushes

You can buy a kit containing everything you need for painting woodwork: usually comprising a 1½-in. or 2-in. paintbrush, plus a paintbrush with angled bristles, used for "cutting in."

Masking Tape

What would we do without this stuff? Masking tape is the only thing to use when painting door or window frames. Simply apply a strip of tape to the edges of the glass to protect against splashes.

Wire brush

This is for cleaning and preparing surfaces for painting—the stiff bristles remove dirt, rust, and paint particles.

28

Stippling brush

Masonry paintbrushes

These are generally quite large and sturdy, with stiff bristles. If the surface to be painted is textured, you will need to use a stippling action rather than a brushing one.

Synthetic bristles

Natural bristles

Roller

For outdoor work, invest in an extension handle, as well—a real back-saver when painting floors and exterior walls. It's sometimes easier to use a roller and extension than to get up on a ladder and use an ordinary roller.

REALLY CAN'T DO WITHOUT

Paint bucket When you're up a ladder, you don't want to have to haul a giant can of paint up with you. Decant it into a smaller can or paint bucket, then hang the bucket from the ladder on a strong wire hook.

Gloves It is always advisable to wear gloves when using exterior paints, since they are not likely to be water-based. Best to avoid getting paint on your hands or you'll have to scrub them and use solvents to get it off.

Razor scraper A handy item if you happen to get a paint splash on your windowpane. It has a metal blade set in a plastic handle—just scrape off the paint without damaging the glass.

CARRY THIS OLD THING UP A LADDER? I DON'T THINK SO!

29

Now for the rough stuff

RAW MATERIALS— ALL ABOUT BRICKS AND PAVING

This is the hard (and the very heavy!) stuff— all the materials to build that barbecue or lay that path or patio. Take a trip to your local hardware store or garden center to check out the variety of slabs, bricks, and blocks available before you plan your project—the staff will be happy to give advice. And don't forget to wear gloves when you start work!

Dependable, solid, and sturdy—just how I like my men to be!

GORGEOUS PAVING SLABS

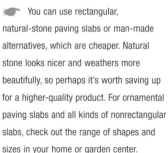

👉 You can use rectangular, natural-stone paving slabs or man-made alternatives, which are cheaper. Natural stone looks nicer and weathers more beautifully, so perhaps it's worth saving up for a higher-quality product. For ornamental paving slabs and all kinds of nonrectangular slabs, check out the range of shapes and sizes in your home or garden center.

BRICKS

👉 Bricks come in all sorts of colors, textures, shapes, and types, depending on the type of clay used in their manufacture and the finishing processes. Mortar, a very fine mix of sharp sand and cement, is used for sticking the bricks together. You can buy it in prepackaged bags of dry mix for convenience—just add water. Bricks basically fall into three categories:

Solid bricks Rectangular, solid bricks, with flat sides all around, though some have a depression called a "frog" on one side. When laid in courses for building, the frog is filled with mortar and acts as a key.

Cored or perforated bricks The same shape as solid bricks, but these bricks have holes right through them. The holes perform the same function as the frog indentation.

Shaped bricks Specially shaped bricks for decorative additions to walls such as corners, arches, wall tops, and so on.

BUILDING BLOCKS

Man-made building blocks are made from poured concrete and are manufactured to various specifications and colors. Some have one textured surface and are used for facing, while others have smooth sides all around for use in general construction. There's a wide variety of blocks to choose from—solid concrete to decorative pierced screen blocks. They are bigger than bricks, so wall construction is quicker!

Non-load-bearing blocks
These are usually used for building internal or dividing walls. They are relatively light, being made from a lightweight aggregate, and can be easily cut and shaped.

Pierced screen (or grille) block
You can build an entire wall using these decorative blocks, or just lay them at intervals for decoration in a solid wall.

Solid structural concrete block
Most often used for the structural core of a building; usually the surface will be faced or rendered on completion. This type of block is dense and quite heavy.

Cored brick

Perforated brick

BRICKS FOR EVERY OCCASION!

Perforated brick

Brick with frog

❋ SORRY MY HANDS ARE A BIT ROUGH, DARLING, BUT I'VE BEEN LAYING THE PATIO...

More raw stuff for fences and pathways

RAW MATERIALS— GRIT, GRAVEL, AND WOOD

Here's an assortment of other materials that you'll find useful when you're being creative with pathways in the yard or when you're fencing yourself in—a kind of sticks-and-stones section. The aggregates are usually sold in big heavy bags, so be careful when lifting them. Most garden centers will have samples for you to have a look at before making your selection.

Lumber

Stronger, thicker, and less flexible than softwood, hardwood lumber is ideal for outdoors. There's a huge range, so ask at the lumberyard which will be best for a particular job.

GET STUCK IN!

FENCE POSTS

A solid fence must be supported by sturdy fence posts. Panel fences require a few square posts anchored to the ground using metal spikes. Chain-link fences work better with specially designed, predrilled concrete or metal posts. Reinforced concrete posts can also be mortised to take horizontal rails or have a vertical groove in which to slot a fence panel.

Round wood fence post A basic type of post for a rustic fencing style. Most wood fence posts you'll find are made from treated softwood, unless you specifically ask for hardwood, which will cost you a lot more money.

Metal fencing spike As an alternative to setting a post in concrete, you can place the lower end of a square fence post into the socket of a big metal spike like this. The spike is driven into the ground using a sledgehammer, then the fence post is inserted.

Square fence post These posts are designed to be used in conjunction with metal fencing spikes and are available in various sizes. They can also be set in concrete as a more permanent installation.

Decking lumber

Fence board

Round wood fence post

Metal fencing spike

Square fence post

CEMENT INGREDIENTS AND AGGREGATES

Concrete consists of portland cement mixed with fine aggregate (sand), coarse aggregate (gravel or crushed stone), and water. When water is added to the dry ingredients, it triggers a chemical reaction in which the cement forms a paste that binds the aggregates into one of the strongest and most versatile of building materials. The ingredients are mixed in different proportions depending on the intended use and desired strength of the concrete. A typical mix consists of 1 part cement, 2½ parts sand, and 3 parts gravel or crushed stone.

Sand

☞ Sand for concrete should be coarse and free of silt and debris. Do not use beach sand or mason's (mortar) sand.

Cement

☞ This looks like a fine gray powder and is sold dry, in great big bags, from hardware stores and home centers.

Gravel

☞ Varies in size, shape, and color. Some are rounded, others sharper and more jagged. Gravel for concrete should be clean and free of debris.

Aggregate

☞ Fine and coarse aggregates (i.e., sand and gravel or crushed stone) for making concrete are sold by the cubic foot or cubic yard. The package information will help you calculate correct quantities.

Post-setting mix

☞ A prepackaged sand, cement, and aggregate dry mix used for setting fence posts in the ground. Insert the post, pack with the dry mix, and add water.

✳ LET ME PUT MY HANDS IN YOUR CEMENT! IT'LL BE JUST LIKE HOLLYWOOD!

All you need for a great exterior

RAW MATERIALS— WET FINISHES

Paints and primers, stains and varnishes—all sorts of wet stuff to prepare, and with which to beautify all your exterior surfaces, from metal to masonry, the deck to the garden shed. You can guarantee there will be a multitude of fabulous products on the market from which to choose. These days loads of new colors and shades are arriving on the shelves all the time. Do not use an indoor product outdoors, because it is not likely to withstand adverse weather conditions and you'll only be disappointed with the result.

Masonry paint

Available in a smooth or textured finish, this is extremely durable, color-fast, and waterproof. It is suitable for all exterior masonry and brickwork.

Exterior enamel paint

This is really tough stuff for exterior woodwork, such as doors and window frames. Some exterior paint products can also be used on metal, downspouts, and gates. It gives a beautiful glossy, hardwearing, weather-resistant finish. It won't last forever, but it will certainly look great for many years.

Paint stripper

Paint strippers are highly caustic chemical substances and must be handled with care. Apply, wait, and watch the paint bubble, then remove it with a scraper. Wear gloves—this stuff will burn your skin.

* NOW IF I WANT A SLEEK, SOPHISTICATED VIBE, I GO FOR TEAK OIL.

TEAK OIL, WOOD STAIN, AND PRIMER

After initial preparation, a good result depends on adequate priming. Whether it is wood, metal, or masonry, each surface should be primed to provide a good base for the topcoat. There are primers suitable both for ferrous (metal that is likely to rust) and nonferrous surfaces (galvanized items, for instance). Just choose the right one for the job. If you don't want to use paint, then try wood stain or furniture oil.

Wood stain Various products are available. Wood stain adds color or wood tones to hard- and softwoods, from fences to sheds and decks. It is designed to protect the wood, yet still allow the beauty of the natural grain to show through.

Teak oil/furniture oil Give your poor old, weather-beaten hardwood furniture a new lease of life with some oil. It replaces the natural essential oils that are necessary to prevent the wood from drying out; it restores the original color, too.

Wood primer All bare wood needs to be primed before beginning the undercoating and painting. The wood primer penetrates the surface of the wood, creates a good base for the topcoats, and ensures better topcoat coverage.

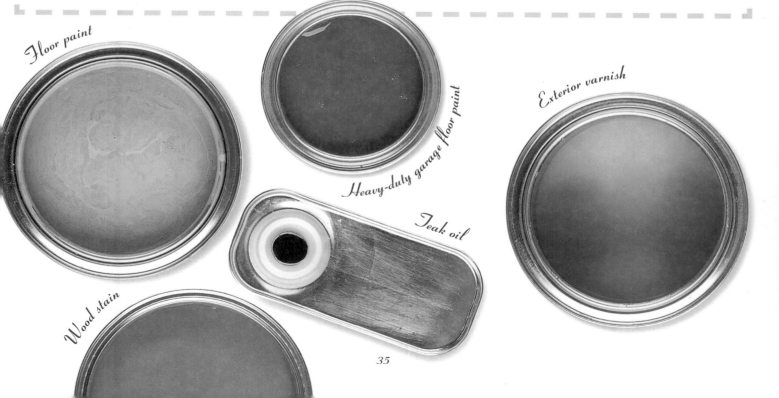

Floor paint

Heavy-duty garage floor paint

Exterior varnish

Teak oil

Wood stain

35

What you need for lighting and water features

SPARKLE AND SPLASH!

SPECIAL-PURPOSE ITEMS— WORKING WITH LIGHT AND WATER

Home improvement antics in the yard do not just include decorating, construction work, and general undergrowth-taming. You could consider your yard to be kind of an outdoor room, complete with running water and lights—be they decorative or functional. Take a look around your local home center. You'll find lots of home improvement kits for lighting and water features such as ponds and sprinklers—you name it. The yard is not just a place to hang your laundry, you know!

Shovel

Useful for shoveling just about anything and for digging holes. It's good to have a matching set of spade and fork.

Edging tool

Use a semicircular blade to dig out electrical-line or water-pipe channels and the pipework channels for sprinkler systems.

OUTDOOR LIGHTS

Decorative lighting Low-voltage lights and solar garden-lighting products are available in great abundance these days. They can be used with delicate tree lights to create a romantic and subtle atmosphere, or as accents along paths or walkways. Simply choose the ones you like best.

Functional lighting You will find a huge range of security-lighting products at any hardware store, from a simple entrance light to a full-scale floodlight kit. You'll surely find something to suit your needs.

Security light

Globe light

Accent light

Note

If you would like a permanent electrical outlet outside, get a professional to install it for you.

Water pump

Water pumps can be bought separately as part of a kit, to create either a water feature or fountain. Water pumps are powered by electricity, which is usually passed through a transformer, reducing the current and making the whole operation safe.

OTHER USEFUL ITEMS

Hand tools For any kind of electrical work, you'll need your screwdriver set and wire cutters or pliers.

Pond liner This is heavy-duty, flexible plastic sheeting, used to line the great big hole that you're going to dig for the pond to house your koi.

Bucket Its purpose is obvious, but do make sure yours doesn't have a hole in it.

Rubber boots Wear good waterproof boots or shoes when working in a watery situation to keep your feet warm and dry.

Mason's line and pins/chalk line For marking out the position of electrical lines or sprinkler-pipe channels.

YOU NEVER KNOW, THERE COULD BE A PALACEFUL OF FROGS UNDER THOSE LILY PADS.

WHEN I SAID I FELT LIKE CHINESE, I MEANT WONTONS WITH NOODLES AND A PILE OF PRAWN CRACKERS...

KISS ME! GO ON, KISS ME! OH, PLEASE! KISS ME!

37

Putting your back into a job without putting pain into your back

LOOKING AFTER YOURSELF IN THE GREAT OUTDOORS

"Lift that barge, tote that bale." There's a right way and a wrong way to do everything, and believe you me you don't want to be doing it the wrong way when there's heavy stuff to lift.

Back injuries are painful and recurring, so please don't take any risks. If you're going to lift a heavy load, never, never bend at the waist, with your legs straight and knees locked. Attempt to lift the load this way and you will injure your back. See the box below for correct lifting procedures!

THIS BEATS DOING SIT-UPS AND PUSH-UPS AT THE GYM!

HOW TO LIFT HEAVY STUFF

☞ Stand close to the object to be lifted and then slowly bend at the knees, keeping your back straight until you are able to grasp the object. Keeping your back as straight as possible, looking directly in front of you, straighten your knees and lift the load. The object is lifted successfully, without sustaining an injury to your back. Never bend forward with your knees straight!

Back
Keep your back straight and never bend forward.

Lifting
When you've loaded the barrow, stand between the handles, bend your knees, and grasp the handles. Then straighten your knees to lift the wheelbarrow off its legs.

Hands
Lifting heavy loads can really chafe your hands, so wear protective gloves!

38

Crowbar

A couple of crowbars are always handy, taking the strain out of prying awkward or heavy objects off, up, or out.

Levers

Here's how a lever works: you have your heavy load, the lever (a plank of wood or a crowbar), and a fulcrum (the point at which the lever pivots). Place the lever on the fulcrum, with one end under the load, while you stand at the other end exerting pressure downward. The result—the load is lifted. Imagine it like a seesaw: when you press down, the load goes up. You can also use a sort of "rowing" action in order to shift the load along bit-by-bit, rather than up.

 **PRACTICAL FASHION**

Clothing For outdoor work in a cold climate, wear thermal underwear to keep you cozy—it also allows free and unrestricted movement of the arms. If you live in a warm and sunny climate, then you can wear a bikini top and shorts, but it's probably best to wear proper pants to protect your skin from scratches and scrapes—and remember the sunscreen. And if you're going to do a lot of painting, invest in some overalls, to save your clothes.

Footwear Wear sturdy boots, preferably with steel toe caps if you are doing anything with heavy stones or pavers.

Accessories Tool belt—a handy little around-the-waist, bits-and-pieces carrier.

Headgear The old favorites: goggles and mask. They are made for comfort and safety—definitely not for style. If in doubt, wear both: it's better to look a fright than have grit in the eye and a lungful of dust. Wear a hard hat, too, if there's a danger of falling objects.

Hands Use the safety gloves for anything that'll be harsh on the mitts. For lighter yard repair, use a good protective hand cream. Then, when you've finished for the day, wash your hands with a heavy-duty hand cleanser to remove any ground-in grime. Next, put on some fragrant hand cream. To prevent dirt from getting stuck inside your nails, scratch a bar of soap before going outside to work. Just wash away later.

Tool bag An invaluable tool-toter.

❋ I ALWAYS RELAX IN THE LOTUS POSITION AFTER A HARD DAY LIFTING TOADSTOOLS.

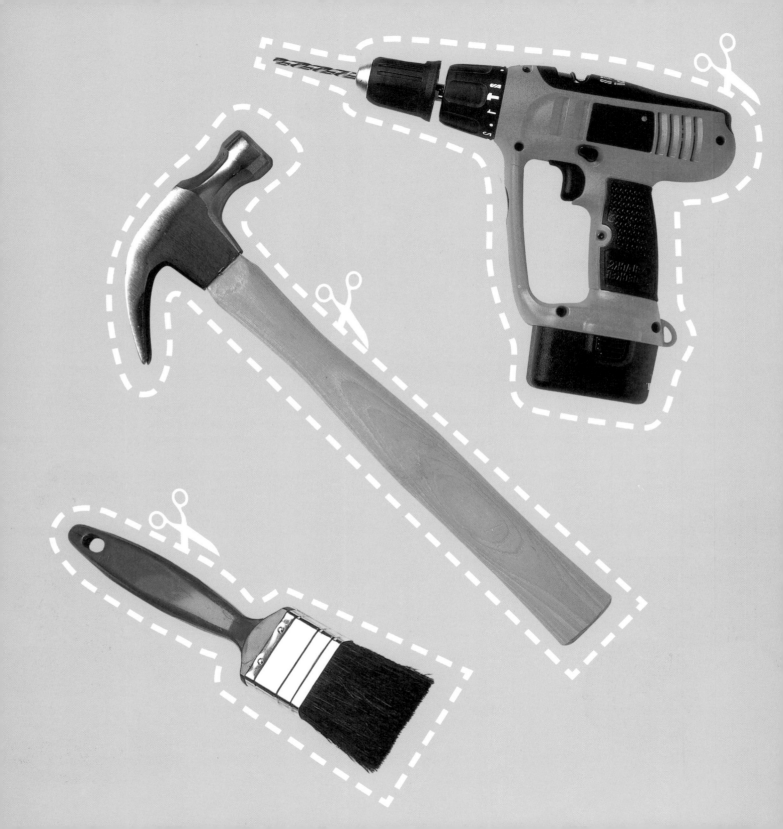

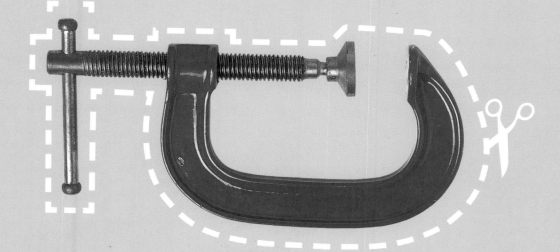

SHEDDING THE LOAD

A place for everything and everything in its place. Good organization really is the key to storage success in the great outdoors.

Storage solutions

STORAGE IN the yard can be a headache sometimes, can't it? Just what do you do with all those cans of paint, garden tools, paintbrushes, watering cans, buckets—need I go on? I'm sure you don't need stuff cluttering up your home, especially if indoor space is at a premium. Find your answer in these simple storage solutions for your garage, shed, and basement. They are very easy to achieve, and the best thing is that they will cost you next to nothing!

USING YOUR SHED EFFECTIVELY

Do you have a neglected shed in your yard? Does it have good storage potential but needs some general maintenance and a bit of cosmetic attention? First, check that the shed is structurally sound—if it really is falling down or unsafe, then demolish it and build a new one on the same base (*see pages 44–47*). However, if it's simply a bit old and tired, then give it a new lease on life. Just grab your tool kit and some paintbrushes.

* BUT WHERE AM I GOING TO PUT THE SAUNA?

* HMM...NOW WHAT TO DO WITH THOSE DUSTY OLD BOOKS?

Never buy stuff that won't fit through the shed door!

QUICK STORAGE MAKEOVER

Preliminary checkup: make sure the shed panels are firmly attached to each other at the corners. If the joints are loose, simply rescrew them securely. Oil the door hinges and replace them if they are rusty. Finally, have a look at the roofing felt: is it secure? Does it leak? If it is loose, reattach it with galvanized nails. If it needs to be replaced, that's easy: just remove the old stuff, buy some new stuff, and attach it with more galvanized nails. Now let's move on to some simple storage solutions.

A GIRL NEEDS ALL THE SUPPORT SHE CAN GET!

1 Simple metal shelf brackets like these are very cheap and readily available just about everywhere. All you have to do is mark the position of your shelf or shelves on the studs (vertical supports) of your shed. Use a level to make sure that the brackets are all at the same height.

2 Now screw the shelf brackets securely in place. Place commercial shelving or a simple piece of wood plank cut to size on the shelf brackets, then screw the bracket to the underside of the shelf just to make sure it will stay put when loaded. You will need one bracket at each end of a short shelf, and one or more in the middle if it's long.

BOOKCASE ORGANIZER

Never throw away an old bookcase! You may not need it in your home anymore, but there will always be a place for it in the shed, garage, or basement. It's a good idea to store your paint cans and solvents away from your living area for safety anyway, so a little shelf unit is just perfect. Load the other shelves with all the other bits and pieces that you don't have space for indoors. You could also screw some small cup hooks or tool-clips to the sides of the bookcase to hold small hand tools or other items.

TWINE DISPENSERS

Another use for those empty jars. Wash and remove the labels, then make a hole through the center of the lids with a hammer and center punch. Place a ball of string or twine in each jar, pass the end through the hole in the lid, and screw the lid back onto the jar. You can now pull the string/twine from the jar when you need it without it getting tangled up.

3 Once the shelf is finished, simply wash and remove the label from all your empty screwtop glass jars, then attach the lids (two screws each) to the underside of your lowest shelf. Fill the jars with screws, nails, and so on, then screw them into the lids. This makes good use of space under shelves, and because you can see through the glass, there's no need for labels. Easy!

43

Construct your own fabulous storage space

BUILDING A SHED FROM A KIT

What? No shed? But it's easy to build one yourself! Most hardware stores and garden centers sell inexpensive sheds in all shapes and sizes. Just measure the space you have available in your yard, then decide which shed would fit it best. It will arrive in giant kit form, and will usually consist of a floor deck, four sides, a roof, a roll of roofing felt, a window, a set of instructions (don't lose these), and a bag of nails, tacks, and screws. The first thing you need to do is read the instructions very carefully and familiarize yourself with all the bits and pieces. Check that everything is present and correct, then begin the assembly. The instructions will tell you exactly which screws and nails to use for each step.

TIP
When laying the paved floor, try to use complete paving slabs so that you won't have to cut them.

1 Prepare the area. This is very important: you can't just build a shed on the bare earth and hope for the best. It needs a dry and solid base to sit on. (Refer to pages 116–17 for leveling ground and page 118 for laying a paved patio.) Basically, a shed floor consists of level, compacted ground with a sheet of landscaping fabric to fend off any weed growth, a layer of sand, and paving slabs on top.

2 The floor of the shed will already have been preconstructed and prepared for you, so all you have to do is position it squarely onto the paving slabs.

3 Place the gabled back and one side panel in position on the shed floor. Drill pilot holes and then screw the lower edges of the side frames to the base, using the large screws provided. Then nail the two panels together at the corner.

4 Install and secure the remaining side panel and the gabled front to the floor in the same way. Screw through to the floor and then nail the panels together at the corner. At each stage check that the corners are at right angles and that the walls are vertical—use a try square and a level.

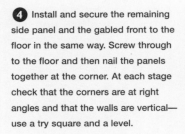

44

TIP
Wear gloves when handling shed panels or you may end up with a sliver.

5 Place the first roof section in position (it doesn't matter which side you do first). Make sure that the top edge is exactly matched up with the peak of the front and back panels. Nail it securely to the shed frame.

6 Next comes the second roof section. This fits onto the shed in exactly the same way as the first. Make sure that the top edge butts neatly against the top edge of the first section at the pea—you don't want any gaps.

need

- gloves
- paving slabs
- landscaping fabric
- sand
- level
- try square
- sledgehammer
- leveling board
- hammer
- galvanized nails
- screwdriver
- drill
- utility knife

7 Using the utility knife, cut two lengths of roofing felt about 4 in. longer than the roof, measuring from front to back. Place one length on the roof, overlapping the peak and protruding beyond the other three edges by about 2 in. Nail roof felt to the frame along the eaves. Space the nails at intervals of about 8 in.

8 Apply the second length of roofing felt in the same way, nailing along the eaves as before. Then nail the overlap securely to the roof near the peaks. Roofing felt is gritty, messy stuff to deal with, so make sure that you brush your clothes off afterward.

IF SHE CAN BUILD A SHED, I SURE CAN, TOO!

9 Nail a corner strip to each of the four corners of the shed. These thin wooden strips finish the construction off nicely and seal the corners against the weather.

10 Fold the edges of the roofing felt neatly at each of the four corners and at the front and back of the peak. You can trim the felt a little at this stage if you've made the overlap too big.

11 Attach the gable trim or rake boards, which are simply boards with mitered ends. Nail two rake boards along the edge of the roof at the front and the back, making sure the mitered ends meet neatly at the peak. The boards hold the edges of the roofing felt securely. To add a touch of individuality, you can use wider boards and cut the edges and ends of the rake boards into a decorative shape.

12 Those two diamond-shaped pieces of wood are called "finials," and are used at the peak of the shed roof at the front and the back. Just hammer them into place using two nails. The purpose of the finials is twofold. They add a decorative finishing touch and they also cover the joint between the rake boards.

✻ SHE SURE HAS A WAY WITH WOOD!

13 The shed kit will not include real glass for the windows; instead, there will be a precut piece of clear acrylic—this is much safer! Place the acrylic into the window frame. It should not need to be trimmed.

46

14 You will have three thin wooden strips left over. These are the glazing strips that will hold the glazing material firmly in the window frame. Place a strip along each side and across the lower edge of the frame, then nail them in place securely.

15 Last but not least, attach the little metal turn button about halfway up the door frame, using the screw provided. This ensures that the shed door will stay firmly shut.

✳ AT LAST, A HOME OF MY OWN!

TOO GOOD JUST TO KEEP TOOLS IN!

AND **PLANNING**

☞ This is a basic tool shed, which you can build yourself. However, you can buy more sophisticated versions. If you live in a climate that is subject to frost or want to attempt a larger, more ambitious project, then be sure to check local building codes first. There may be specific codes regarding positioning and foundations, so you may need a permit before you proceed. You don't want to build a magnificent masterpiece and then have to make it smaller or demolish it!

Cosmetic surgery for sheds MORE MORE MORE

PAINTING A SHED 2

All exterior wood needs to be protected from the elements with stain, paint, or a wood sealant. Exterior-quality wood finishes are available in many fabulous colors. I chose wood stains in subtle blues and sage green. The wax-enriched formula is quick-drying, water-repellent, and not harmful to plants or pets. It can be used on fences and rough-sawn exterior woodwork, too. Load a paintbrush well, and apply the stain in thick, even coats. Do not spread the stain out too much, as this can result in a patchy finish. Paint all the stripes in one color first, then proceed with the next color. One coat should be enough, but if it needs another when the stain is dry, simply recoat in the same way.

FITTING A NEW LOCK 3

☛ If you are using your shed to store tools or other valuable items, you will need to consider security. A simple hasp and staple, along with a sturdy padlock should be enough to keep the shed secure and act as a deterrent to casual intruders.

need
* hasp and staple with screws
* padlock
* awl
* screwdriver

1 Mark the position of the hasp on the door, then mark the position of the staple in a corresponding position on the door frame. Make pilot holes for the screws in the wood with an awl. It is vital for the two parts to line up exactly or you will have difficulty closing the hasp over the staple.

2 Screw both parts securely into position. Close the hasp onto the staple then pass the padlock through it. A locking device like this is quite secure, because when closed, the screw heads are completely covered, thus making them more difficult to remove.

MAKING A WINDOW BOX

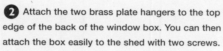

OK, maybe this is a bit extravagant, but it is a cute finishing touch. Fill window boxes with real or fake flowers, depending on whether you like high- or low-maintenance gardening!

1 For the window box, simply cut three pieces of lumber a little longer than the width of the window, and cut two more pieces to about 4 in. in length. Screw the two short-end pieces to two of the long pieces to form the sides (drill pilot holes first). Then screw the last piece to the base to complete the box.

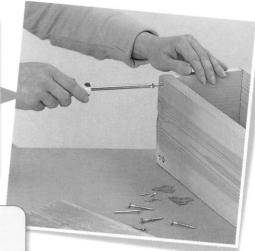

2 Attach the two brass plate hangers to the top edge of the back of the window box. You can then attach the box easily to the shed with two screws.

need

* scraps of 1-in. x 6-in. lumber
* drill
* screws
* brass plate hangers
* screwdriver

* DO YOU THINK GEORGE WILL RUN UP SOME DRAPES FOR ME IF I ASK NICELY?

ADDING DRAPES

☛ Drapes are a nice finishing touch to your shed. Cut two pieces of fabric as wide as the window and about 12 in. longer than the height. Stitch a narrow double hem down both sides of both pieces, then fold and stitch a ¾-in. double hem across the top and bottom edges. Cut a piece of curtain wire a little shorter than the width of the window and screw an eye to each end. Pass the wire though the top hem of each drape. Screw the hook to each side of the top of the window frame on the inside, then hang up the drapes. If you like, you could also make some tie-backs from strips of fabric or ribbons.

need

* pretty drape fabric
* curtain wire
* two screwhooks and eyes
* scissors, pins, thread, etc.

A girl just can't have too many shelves

PUTTING UP ADJUSTABLE SHELVES

5

Adjustable shelving is a perfect way to make the best use of wall space in your garage or basement because you can adjust the size to suit your storage needs. A wide range of adjustable shelving systems are available from home centers or hardware stores. All you have to do is secure the shelving standards in position and then add the shelving brackets where desired!

1 Consider your wall area and decide where you'd like the shelves to be. If you are attaching the shelves to a frame house, bear in mind that the standards should be screwed into studs. One major consideration is height: you need to be able to reach them easily. Mark the position of each standard with a faint pencil line and use a level to make sure that it's straight. Then mark the top of each standard—again, use the level to make sure the marks are horizontal.

2 Place one standard in position. Mark the position of the topmost screw. Drill a hole at the mark and insert a wall anchor. Loosely drive a screw through the standard's top hole into the anchor. Make sure the standard is vertical and then mark the other screw hole positions. Do this with all the standards in turn.

3 Gently swing the standard out of the way, then drill a hole at each marked position. Insert a wall anchor into each hole.

4 Screw all the standards securely to the wall. Remember to tighten the topmost screw. You can now insert all the shelving brackets. Each one has a shaped end that hooks onto the standards and supports the shelves at the height required.

need

* drill
* wall anchors
* screws
* screwdriver
* level
* pencil
* shelving standards
* shelving brackets
* shelves

PUTTING UP A PEGBOARD WALL PANEL

Perforated hardboard, or "pegboard," has small predrilled holes all over it. Buy wire hooks in all shapes and sizes, then organize them as you please on the pegboard to hold tools and equipment.

need

* drill
* wall anchors
* screws
* screwdriver
* level
* pencil
* sheet pegboard
* chrome washers

1 Hold the panel up to the wall, then mark the corner position of the pegboard panel on the wall with faint pencil lines.

2 Mark, drill, and anchor screw holes at each corner and at 8-in. intervals along each side. Ensure that the marks correspond with the predrilled holes in the board along the sides. Now slip a washer onto each screw before securing the panel to the wall.

PUTTING UP BIKE/LADDER HOOKS

Large heavy-duty hooks are the only way to hang up heavy items like ladders or bicycles. They come in various sizes to suit all needs. Simply secure the hooks in a suitable position, then hang up your stuff.

need

* drill
* wall anchors
* screws
* screwdriver
* level
* pencil
* heavy-duty ladder/bike hooks

1 Mark the position of each hook using a level. Each hook must be at the same height as its partner so that your bike or ladder will hang straight. If the hooks are widely spaced, use a long wooden strip to span the area between the marks, then place the level on top of the strip.

2 Hold the hook up to the wall and mark each screw hole with a pencil dot. Drill the holes, drive in anchors, then screw the hook into place. Secure the other hook/hooks in position to complete your hanging system.

TIP
For drilling screw holes in masonry, use a masonry bit and insert a wall anchor into the hole. If you insert screws directly into the wall, they will come loose in no time.

More storage

ADDING TOOL HOOKS TO PEGBOARD

8

Your outdoor tools may be large and cumbersome, and even a bit grubby, so you wouldn't really want to drag them inside your house and ruin your interior home improvement! Adding tool hooks is the perfect way to organize outdoor tools in your shed, garage, or basement.

1 Insert the tool hooks into the pegboard panel. Each hook will have two prongs especially for this purpose. You may have to squeeze the prongs together a little to fit them into the holes.

2 Place the hooks in a row at intervals of about 2 in. to accommodate garden tool handles. Hooks like these are available in all shapes and sizes; simply choose those that suit your needs.

need
* long pegboard tool hooks

WHEELBARROW STORAGE

9

☞ What do you do with a wheelbarrow when it's not in use? Park it in the yard upside down and you're likely to trip over it. Why not hang it up? Use pieces of scrap wood to make this simple hanging device.

1 Using a tenon saw, cut 13¾-in. lengths of 1-in. x 1-in. and 1-in. x 2-in. lumber (one each). Glue and screw the pieces together to form an L-shape to hold the base of the wheelbarrow. Now cut a piece of 1-in. x 2-in. lumber to fit between the handles of the wheelbarrow.

2 Cut two shorter pieces to act as turn buttons to hold the handles. Screw the turn buttons to the larger piece, as shown.

3 Mark the position of both parts of the wheelbarrow holder on the wall. Drill and anchor, then screw the pieces into place. Hang up the wheelbarrow by placing the edge of the pan in the lower L-shape, then rest the handles on the wall (on either side of the upper holder). Swivel the turn buttons to hold the handles.

need
* drill and wall anchors
* screwdriver and screws
* level and pencil
* scraps of 1-in. x 2-in. lumber
* scraps of 1-in. x 1-in. lumber
* tenon saw and wood glue

MAKING GALVANIZED MESH STORAGE BOXES

Galvanized metal or mesh is ideal for use indoors and outdoors because it is rustproof. Also, if you use these boxes to store stuff outside, they don't fill with water.

10

need

* one sheet of galvanized 1-in. wire mesh, about 2 ft. x 3 ft.
* side cutter

1 Place the mesh sheet on a flat surface, then work from one short side inward. Using the side cutter, snip a slot that is one square wide and nine squares long, about five squares in from the edge.

2 Fold up the two long side sections of the mesh sheet at right angles to the base, then fold in the end pieces at right angles to the sides. This forms the basic rectangular form of the box.

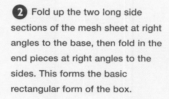

3 Fold the remaining ends around the short sides, then tuck them inside. Your wonderful new storage box will now hold its shape quite securely without extra fastenings.

* YES! YES! YES! RUST-FREE STORAGE AT LAST!

AND YOU THOUGHT BASKETWORK WAS JUST FOR THERAPY!

TIP
Avoid using cardboard boxes, especially for storage in the shed or a damp environment. Cardboard will absorb moisture and become soft—a problem when you lift it up and the bottom falls out!

MORE
STORAGE IDEAS

Keep your eyes peeled for other boxes that may be cheap or free! Your local market may throw away light, plywood orange boxes regularly. Simply rescue them from the garbage and then paint with the color of your choice. Great for storing bits and pieces.

Junk potting table

THIS OLD sideboard was an irresistible yard-sale find. I just fell in love with its cool retro shape and thought it would look perfect in the yard as a potting table and storage cabinet in one. This kind of transformation is frighteningly easy, girls. All you have to do is add a coat of colorful exterior paint to protect the wood from the elements, then make a shiny, new aluminum cover for the top. To complete, just screw a few large hooks in each side to hang your hand tools or gloves on. You can chalk "yard repairs to do" lists on the chalkboard doors or draw little pictures to remind you of what's been stored inside.

FROM JUNK TO JEWEL IN NO TIME!

1 Remove the doors and drawers, then sand all surfaces thoroughly to remove old varnish and to create a good base for paint. Use an electric sander to make your job easier (sanding is hard work).

need

* junk cabinet or sideboard
* sander and dust mask
* mineral spirits
* soft cloth
* primer
* exterior paint
* chalkboard paint
* paintbrush and gloves
* piece of thin aluminum
* utility knife
* metal ruler
* tin snips
* wood strip
* center punch
* awl
* hammer
* four domed chrome screws
* four chrome washers
* screwdriver
* screw hooks

2 Remember that sanding is a very dusty activity, so wear a protective mask. When you've finished the job, wipe all the surfaces clean with a cloth or rag soaked in mineral spirits.

3 Apply a coat of primer to the bare wood on the sideboard carcass and the door and drawer fronts. When the primer is dry, paint the carcass and the small cabinet doors with green exterior paint and the large doors and drawer fronts with chalkboard paint. Allow all the paint to dry, then apply a second coat if necessary.

4 Ask your local metal supplier to cut a piece of thin aluminum for you that overlaps the top of the old cabinet or sideboard by approximately 1 in. all around. Measure, mark, and score a line 1 in. in from each side of the metal rectangle. Use a utility knife and a metal ruler to do this.

5 Snip into the corner as shown, then bend the metal along the score lines using a wood strip as a guide. It's a good idea to wear gloves while you do this to keep you from cutting your fingers. Bend all four sides to shape in this way, making sure that the corners are folded in neatly.

☀ HOW NICE IS THIS? GO ON, MAKE YOUR OWN!

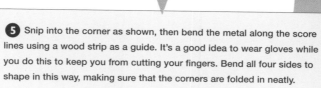

6 Place the metal worktop in position on the sideboard. Punch holes through the metal at each corner, using the hammer and center punch. Then pierce a pilot hole for the screw in the wood underneath using an awl.

7 Slip a chrome washer onto each of the chrome screws, then secure the top in place by screwing through the holes into the sideboard frame. Finally, remove the protective plastic film from the metal worktop and screw a few large hooks to each side to dangle your hand tools from. Use colored chalk to draw a few pretty pictures on the doors just for fun!

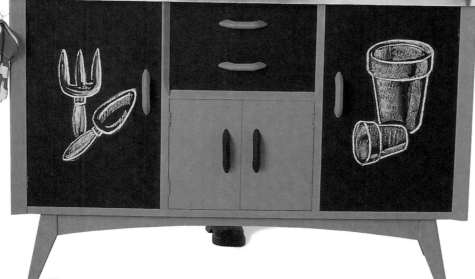

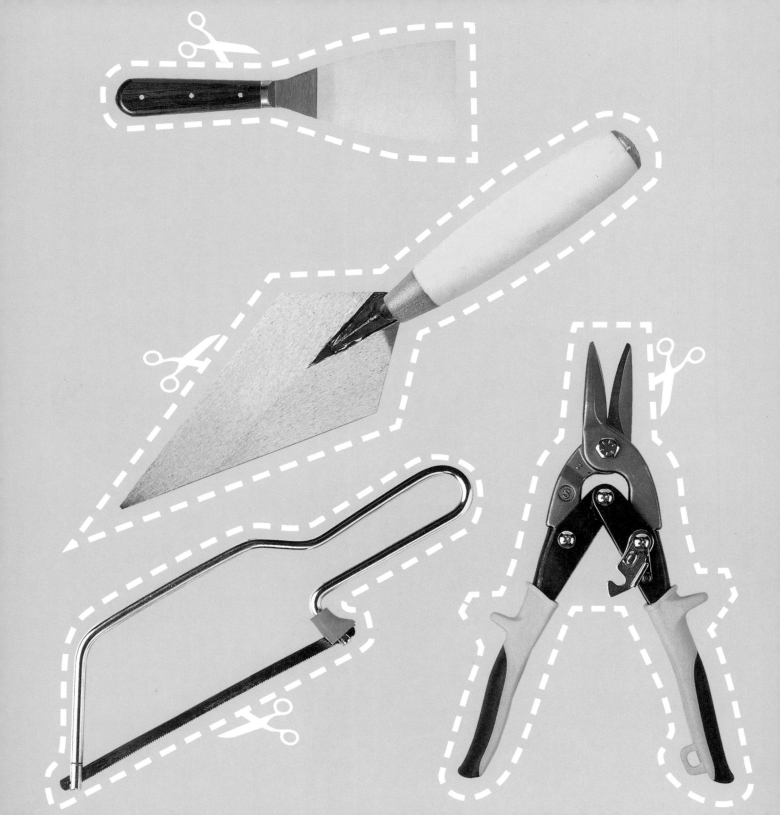

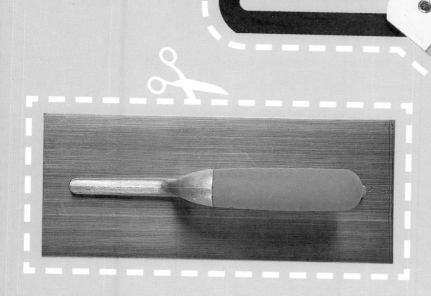

KEEPING UP APPEARANCES

Basic fixes for exteriors, from roofs and drains to walls and windows, plus lots of little extras that you might find useful in the great outdoors.

Head to toe exterior maintenance

Prevention is, as always, better than cure. Solve small problems before they become big ones: locate loose tiles, find problematic downpipes, and clear minor blockages in drains before they turn into major ones. Regular maintenance can save you money in the long run. This section shows you that simple exterior maintenance isn't as scary as it looks—you'll be replacing downspouts, renovating siding, attaching storm windows, fitting an outdoor faucet and much, much more—and still have time to paint your nails afterward.

HELLO, ROOF!

It's worth investing in a pair of binoculars. Why? Well, every now and then (twice a year should suffice), they will enable you to take a close look at the condition of your roof from the safety of terra firma. Spot small problems before they get out of hand: loose tiles, wobbly downpipes, and so on. Make inspections after storms or bad weather, because strong winds tend to lift tiles or shingles, which in turn allows water to penetrate the roof cavity.

* DON'T GO LOOKING WHERE YOU SHOULDN'T BE LOOKING!

ROOFING MATERIALS AND FORMS

Asphalt shingles are one of the most common roofing materials, but slate and clay tiles are also prized for their strength and durability. Concrete tiles are a lighter, cheaper alternative to slate or clay. Wood shingles or slates are popular, but require a lot of maintenance.

Bonnet hip tiles
* Curved to fit around the outside edge of a roof hip.

Standard tiles
* Cover most of the roof. They are slightly convex and have nail holes along the top edge.

Ridge and hip tiles
* Curvy or pointy, they cover the gap where roof slopes meet at the top (ridge) or side (hip).

Valley tiles
* Cover where two slopes meet at the bottom.

ANATOMY OF A ROOF

In its most basic form, an ordinary gable roof is triangular in shape, which is a good load-bearing shape. The weight of the roof is carried by sloping rafters that meet at the peak of the roof, the "ridge." To keep the roof from pushing out the walls of the house, the bases of the rafters are joined together horizontally by joists. However, most roofs have additional hipped ends, dormer windows, or extended parts, making them quite complicated structures. The diagram shows a typical roof with hips, ridges, valleys, and various other features. The cross section shows a simple three-layer construction: rafters first, then roofing felt, then roofing strips to hold the felt secure, and finally roof coverings—tiles, shingles, and so on. There are a few danger spots to keep a careful eye on: flashings around chimneys or dormer windows, valleys in which one plane of the roof meets another, and ridges or hipped ends on which the tiles might slip or be lifted by the wind. Be vigilant, and you won't have too much to worry about.

FLASHINGS

☞ A few words about flashings. These are strips of material—most commonly copper, galvanized steel, or aluminum—used to weatherproof the joints between the roof and other parts. You'll find flashing strips along valleys and abutments between chimneys, dormers, and walls, and where one roof meets another. They can wear out or sustain damage over the years, causing leaks. Replacement flashing is readily available from home centers in order to make small repairs.

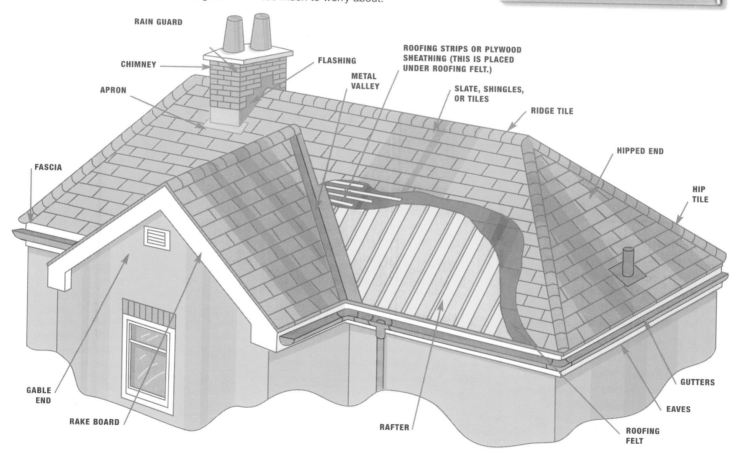

RAIN GUARD

CHIMNEY

APRON

FLASHING

ROOFING STRIPS OR PLYWOOD SHEATHING (THIS IS PLACED UNDER ROOFING FELT.)

METAL VALLEY

SLATE, SHINGLES, OR TILES

RIDGE TILE

HIPPED END

HIP TILE

FASCIA

GABLE END

RAKE BOARD

RAFTER

GUTTERS

EAVES

ROOFING FELT

Letting yourself loose up on the roof

REPLACING A LOOSE SLATE

A slate may work itself loose due to a break or crack, or perhaps the fixing nails have corroded, allowing it to slip. Replace it immediately—high winds love to work their way under a loose slate and strip it and its neighbors right off. Any material has a limited life, so if your roof is old and in bad shape then small repairs should only be considered as a temporary fix while you save up for a full or partial replacement. If you do decide to make a repair, try to use a slate that matches the existing ones as closely as possible.

SPOTTING LEAKS

Leaks are a common problem for homeowners. Sometimes the causes and remedies are clear, but at other times the sources of leaks will be a little elusive and you will have to resort to detective work. Camp out in the attic on a rainy day (a flashlight helps), and wait and watch. Eventually you'll discover where the water is coming in. It might not be obvious: water can be sneaky. When the source has been identified, you can get started fixing the leak. Always try to repair a small leak before it gets to be a deluge—it won't go away if you ignore it!

1 Use a slate ripper to cut and remove the nails that hold the slate in place. Slip the tool under the broken tile and hook the end around the nail. Hammer on the slate ripper's knee to try to either remove the nail or cut through it. If the slate has slipped off by itself, you will need to remove old nails anyway before you can insert the new one.

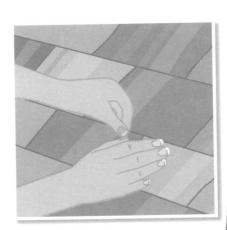

3 Position the new slate on top of the copper strip, then slide it into place. The lower edge of the new tile should match up exactly with the edges of the tiles on each side so that it doesn't look out of line. When you are satisfied with the positioning, you can fold the end of the copper strip over the lower edge of the slate to hold it securely.

2 Remove the old, damaged slate. It won't be possible for you to nail the new slate into position, so get a copper strip about 1 in. longer than the depth of the slate. Nail the top end of the strip to the roofing strips underneath. To do this the nail must pass through the gap between the tiles on the previous course.

THIS ISN'T THE PLACE FOR HIGH HEELS!

need
* slate ripper
* hammer
* copper strip
* nails
* new slate

REPAIRING A BROKEN TILE

13

A broken or cracked tile may be a bit tricky to remove. The molded interlocking or overlapping shape of each tile has little retaining "nibs" on the back. These nibs hold the tiles securely in position, but also make them difficult to remove! Use a few wooden wedges to make the task easier.

need
* new tile
* wooden wedges
* slate ripper

Who would have thought wedges could be so useful?

14

REPLACING ASPHALT SHINGLES

Asphalt shingles are one of the most common roofing materials, and they come in a variety of colors. Curled or slightly torn shingles can be repaired by gluing them down with roofing cement and reinforcing them with galvanized roofing nails.

❶ Carefully lift the uppermost good shingle using a pry bar. Remove the first row of nails that are holding down the damaged shingle by slipping the pry bar underneath the damaged shingle and pulling upward. After removing the nails, gently pull out the broken shingle pieces. Slide the new shingle up into place and align it carefully with the neighboring shingles.

❷ When the new shingle is in position, carefully secure it in place with four galvanized roofing nails. Use the pry bar to hammer the new nails into position—this allows you to drive in the new nail without damaging or bending the shingles above. Place the pry bar over the top of the nail head and hammer on the pry bar a few inches down and away from the upper shingle.

❶ Locate the offending tile. If it is in an overlapping pattern (as pictured), you will need to raise the tiles on either side. If it is interlocking, then you may also have to raise the one above and to the left.

❷ To remove the tile you will need to ease it up from the roofing strip on which it rests. Drive wooden wedges gently under the surrounding tiles, then try to ease the broken one free. If it's attached with a nail, then you will need to either wiggle it loose or cut it, using a slate ripper to free the tile. Now insert a new tile into the gap and remove the wedges.

* THIS IS AS HIGH AS I LIKE TO GET!

Keeping it all covered

REPLACING A BUILT-UP FLAT ROOF

15

Flat roofs can sometimes be problematic for the people who live underneath them. Traditional asphalt-saturated roofing felt tends to become brittle with age, and leaks can be difficult to detect on flat roofs because the water can run downhill from the entry point before seeping through. A major replacement job for a house should be left to the professionals, but a flat roof on a small shed or garage should be within your reach. The materials you need are readily available from hardware stores or home centers, sometimes in kit form. Keep an eye on the forecasts because you'll need dry, calm weather for this job. Begin by removing the old felt. This is messy and dusty work, so wear protective gloves and a mask. The felt is built up in three layers, two of felt and one of mineral felt-top.

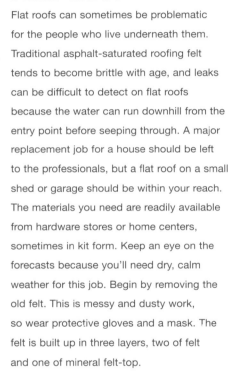

✳ DISCOVER A WHOLE NEW MEANING TO "GETTING HAMMERED!"

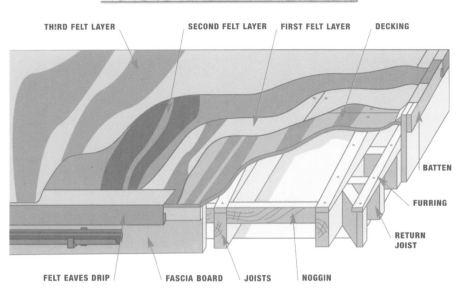

FLAT ROOF STRUCTURE

THIRD FELT LAYER · SECOND FELT LAYER · FIRST FELT LAYER · DECKING

BATTEN

FURRING

RETURN JOIST

FELT EAVES DRIP · FASCIA BOARD · JOISTS · NOGGIN

☞ Wood-framed flat roofs are often found on rear extensions, sheds, and garages. Sturdy joists cross the shorter spans at intervals of about 18 in. The ends of the joists are attached to wall plates on load-bearing walls, or set into the brickwork of an extension with metal hangers. Flat roofs aren't completely level: they must be slightly sloped to allow rainwater to run off. If the slope isn't sufficient, standing water can seep through. Roofers achieve this slight slope by nailing long, tapered "furrings" to the top edges of the joists, meaning that the roof slopes a little but the ceiling inside is flat—clever! Decking lies on top of the sloping wood framework: a simple plywood or prefelted chipboard layer about ¾ in. thick is nailed to the joists, providing a flat surface for the layers of roofing felt. The short lengths of wood between the joists are called "noggins" and give extra support to the edges. Sometimes a layer of light-colored gravel or crushed stone is placed on top of the final layer of roofing felt in order to provide extra weatherproofing and reflect the sun's rays, lowering the temperature inside the building.

Claw hammer

IT'S A TOUGH PROBLEM THAT CAN'T BE CRACKED WITH A HAMMER!

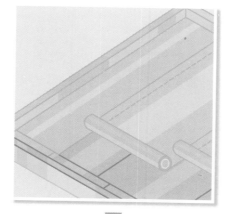

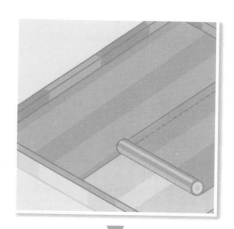

1 Apply a strip of felt one-third the width of the roll all around and over the built-up edges of the roof. Cover the decking with the remaining strips of two-thirds width, then use whole widths. Overlap each piece by 4 in. Nail through the center of the overlaps, then trim the edge flush to the eaves. Cut a strip of felt and wrap it around the eaves to form a "drip" covering the edge. Snip and fold neatly at the corners, then nail into place.

2 For the second layer, cut enough pieces of felt to fit the width of the roof and glue them to the first layer using cold asphalt adhesive applied with a brush. Overlap each piece, fold and tuck around the built-up edges, then add a drip to the eaves. To glue the pieces down, put them in position and roll up half of the strip, apply the adhesive to the first layer, unroll, and press flat, then roll up the other half and glue in the same way.

3 Cut and lay the mineral felt-top layer in the same way as the second layer, but lap it over the eaves drips rather than the built-up edges. Finally, cut mineral felt-top strips and nail and glue them in place around the sides and rear edges.

need

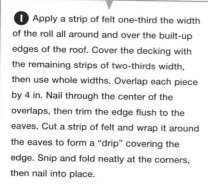

* rolls of roofing felt
* mineral felt-top layer
* ladder
* claw hammer
* galvanized roofing nails
* cold asphalt adhesive
* gloves
* mask
* utility knife
* soft flat-soled shoes
* lots of strong bags for the old roofing felt

SURE I'D LOVE TO HELP, BUT I MIGHT RUIN MY NICE NEW JACKET!

REPAIRING

SPLITS AND CRACKS

Localized splits and cracks can easily be fixed by applying some self-adhesive, roof-repair tape. Clear the roof of any dirt or debris first and use a fungicide to get rid of moss or lichen. If the crack is quite long, stick one end of the tape to the roof and unroll the tape, pressing down as you go. As an added precaution, a liquid waterproof treatment can be applied to the entire surface, using a roller with an extended handle. Three coats will give a good weatherproof layer. Try to check the roof once or twice a year. Remove debris and wash away any mold. Note areas in which water is accumulating; they may lead to leaks in the future.

Getting down and dirty up on the roof

CLEARING A BLOCKED GUTTER

16

A blocked gutter will eventually cause water to overflow, which in turn may lead to moisture problems in the surrounding walls. The weight of standing water in plastic guttering systems can also cause distortion, over time leading to splits and cracks.

1 Make sure that the base of the ladder is on level ground and that the top is propped solidly against the wall or roof fascia. Don't place the top of the ladder on plastic or aluminum gutters because this can cause damage. Hang your bucket from one of the top rungs using a paint-can hook, leaving both hands free.

2 Block the drop outlet with old rags so that the blockage doesn't fall through the downspout instead! Inspect the gutter along its length to locate the blockages. Clear any stubborn accumulations with a trowel or plastic scraper.

3 Put on your rubber gloves and scoop up the debris, placing it in the bucket. When you are satisfied that the system is free from all obstructions, remove the rags from the outlet and pour a bucket of fresh water down the pipe to flush it.

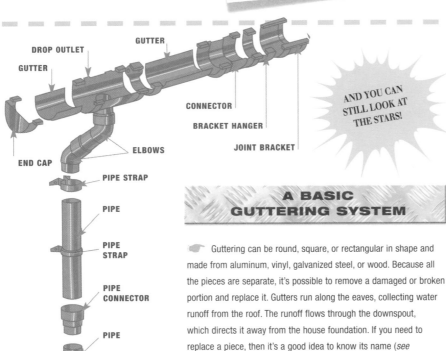

DROP OUTLET
GUTTER
GUTTER
CONNECTOR
BRACKET HANGER
JOINT BRACKET
END CAP
ELBOWS
PIPE STRAP
PIPE
PIPE STRAP
PIPE CONNECTOR
PIPE

AND YOU CAN STILL LOOK AT THE STARS!

A BASIC GUTTERING SYSTEM

☞ Guttering can be round, square, or rectangular in shape and made from aluminum, vinyl, galvanized steel, or wood. Because all the pieces are separate, it's possible to remove a damaged or broken portion and replace it. Gutters run along the eaves, collecting water runoff from the roof. The runoff flows through the downspout, which directs it away from the house foundation. If you need to replace a piece, then it's a good idea to know its name (*see diagram*). Some of the pieces are not symmetrical, so you'll also need to note the direction of any bends before you buy new pieces.

need

* rubber gloves
* ladder
* bucket
* hook

FIXING A LOOSE DOWNSPOUT 17

After years of wear and tear, your poor old downspout can get a bit loose and wobbly. Straps can become brittle and crack, and screws can work loose. If the pipes are not held rigidly in place, over time the joints in the downspout can leak. Leaky downspouts cause damage to brickwork and pointing, and penetrating water will eventually give rise to serious moisture problems.

1 First, locate the offending pipe straps. If a strap has worked loose and the pipe moves a lot, then it will probably have caused a few others to loosen, too. Wobble the pipe around a bit to see if they are attached firmly. Use a securely positioned ladder to gain access to the high straps. Loosen the screws with the screwdriver, then remove the old strap and discard—do not try to reuse an old strap.

TIP
You can fit a plastic leaf-guard to the top of a downspout to keep out leaves and discourage birds from setting up home there.

WALL ANCHORS

Screws won't hold fast in solid masonry or brick. If you just drill a hole and insert the screw, then it will work loose and come out again in no time. You need to use wall anchors. These are tubes of plastic that are inserted into the predrilled screw hole. When the screw is driven in, the tube expands, gripping the inside of the hole and holding the screw secure. Choose an anchor to match the size of screw you're using. Check the manufacturers' guidelines first.

Wall anchors

2 It might be necessary to replace the wall anchors if they are damaged. If so, just pull them out using long-nose pliers and insert new ones of the same size into the old holes. Tap the new wall anchor into place with a small hammer.

3 If the masonry has crumbled, it's a good idea to drill and anchor a new hole in a slightly different position. Insert new wall anchors then position the new strap around the downspout, aligning the holes with the wall anchor holes, and screw securely in place.

* WHEN I FIX YOUR PIPE STRAPS, THEY STAY FIXED!

need
* new pipe strap
* screws to fit
* screwdriver
* new wall anchors
* ladder if needed
* drill with masonry bit if needed
* long-nose pliers

Cure those leaky downspouts

REPLACING A SECTION OF DOWNSPOUT

18

Splits and damaged areas in plastic downspouts can have a number of causes. Plastic is not as strong as galvanized steel, for example, so if a ladder is propped against a plastic gutter, it is likely to damage it. Another cause of damage is snow and ice, especially if the gutter or downspout is blocked with debris. The standing water in the pipe can freeze and expand, causing distortion that leads to more serious problems if left unchecked.

※ BELIEVE ME, THE RUMORS ABOUT MY DAMAGED DOWNSPOUT ARE GREATLY EXAGGERATED!

1 Use a securely positioned ladder to reach the damaged area safely. When you have found the damage in a downspout, loosen all the straps that hold it in place. Use your tool belt to hold any tools you need for the job, leaving both hands free. Remove the damaged piece and discard it; you may have to cut out a section using the hacksaw.

TIP

It's always better to replace a broken or damaged section of pipe than to try to repair it.

2 Measure the length of the replacement piece and mark it on the new pipe. Clamp the pipe securely on your workbench and saw the pipe to size. It should be easy to make a straight cut, but if you have problems, just tape a sheet of paper around the pipe, aligning the edges, and use it as a cutting guide.

need

* ladder
* new section of downspout
* pipe connector if necessary
* large hacksaw
* workbench
* steel tape
* new pipe straps

You can get special paint for plastic downspouts too!

3 If you have removed a portion of a long piece of pipe, you need to slip a pipe connector onto the ends of the old pipe and slot in the new part. The connectors will form sound, watertight joints. When you are satisfied with the job, replace all the pipe straps and check once more that the pipe is securely attached to the wall.

INSTALLING A RAIN BARREL

19

In times of increased demand, it makes sense to save every drop of water we can and use it for our thirsty gardens or potted plants when the weather is dry. A rain barrel or rainwater diverter is the obvious way to save natural rainwater; the runoff from the roof amounts to a huge volume of water over time. These receptacles are available in various sizes.

1 Stand the rain barrel in a firm and level position near the downspouts and remove the lid. Make one mark on the pipe at the same height as the top of the rain barrel; you can use a level for this. Make a second mark between 4 in. and 5 in. above the first, depending on the downspout diameter. The instructions will indicate the correct measurement.

2 Use a hacksaw to cut the downspout carefully along the lines marked. Remove the cut-out section and discard it. Try the diverter for size in the downspout and cut where indicated in the instructions, using the utility knife to fit.

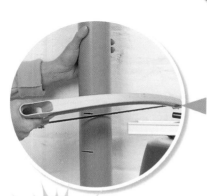

Position the rain barrel in a cool, shady place; if it gets warm the water will evaporate.

3 Place the top section of the diverter in the downspout threaded-side down, then slide the pipe up a little and hold it in position. Place the lower section in position threaded-side up. Screw the assembly together and then allow the unit to fall into the lower part of the downspout.

HOW BIG DO YOU WANT YOUR BUTT TO BE, MA'AM?

4 Cut a 1-in. diameter hole in the side of the rain barrel, placing the top of the hole about 5 in. below the top of the barrel. Fit the connector washer and nut to the barrel, then join the diverter to the barrel with the flexible hose provided.

need

* large hacksaw
* marker pen and level
* measuring tape
* rainwater diverter kit
* utility knife
* rain barrel and stand

Cleaning exterior walls with style

USING A POWER WASHER

20

All you need is a power supply and a water supply. Attach your hose to an exterior (or interior) tap, then attach the other end to the washer. Plug the unit into an electrical outlet using an outdoor extension cord. Switch on the water, then the power, and off you go. The washer nozzle is adjustable, so you can have a fine jet or a spray. Hold the nozzle about 8–10 in. away from the dirty surface for the best results.

need

* power washer
* garden hose
* rubber boots
* rubber gloves
* fungicidal solution

ONCE YOU START, YOU WON'T BE ABLE TO STOP!

1 Stuccoed and painted portions of exterior walls accumulate dirt and mud splashes from rain and human or motor traffic. These eyesores are easily removed with a power washer. Just blast away the dirt, grime, and peeling paint, then repaint when dry.

2 Here, the brickwork around a leaky drain pipe has become damp and acquired a mold growth. If left untreated this would spread. Remove the mold with a power washer, then apply a fungicidal solution with a brush or sponge. After four hours, rinse the area with clean water—and don't forget to repair the leaky pipe!

* STAND BACK! ONCE I POWER UP, THERE'S NO STOPPING ME!

GETTING RID OF EFFLORESCENCE
21

☞ Efflorescence occurs when salts in the bricks gradually migrate to the surface as the wall dries. Wearing a dust mask, brush the affected area with a dry, stiff household brush. Eventually all the salts will have been expelled from the brickwork and the problem will disappear. Be careful not to use excessive pressure if the brick surface is delicate, because this can cause damage.

need

* stiff household brush
* dust mask

USING CHEMICAL PRODUCTS

While you're in exterior clean-up mode, you might discover that a previous occupant has been a bit careless and dripped paint on the brickwork. Annoying, but not irreversible. Careful application of an ordinary paint remover will do the trick, leaving your brickwork nice and clean. Bear this in mind if you decide to repaint the exterior. Try not to splash paint around in a haphazard fashion—it just makes more work for you to do later on.

1 Wearing your rubber gloves, decant some paint remover into a paint bucket. Use a small paintbrush to apply the product, dabbing it into the surface thoroughly. Wait for about ten minutes or as the manufacturer directs.

* I MAY BE STRONGER, BUT SHE'S BETTER AT STRIPPING!

TIP
Paint removers/strippers are highly toxic and give off unpleasant fumes. It is best to wear a mask when using these products.

2 The chemical stripper will dissolve and soften the paint until it is ready for removal. Remove thick residues with a paint scraper and scrub smaller areas using an old toothbrush. Repeat the process if any paint particles are left in crevices or buried deep in textured surfaces. It's worth taking time to make sure that all the paint particles are removed.

need
* paint remover
* paint bucket
* rubber gloves
* paintbrush
* old toothbrush
* household brush
* paint scraper

SAFETY

☞ Never direct the washer jet at people or animals.

☞ Always wear protective gloves when using paint removal and stripping products because they are extremely caustic and will burn you if they come into contact with your skin.

3 Finally, when you are satisfied, rinse the whole area with clean water. Use a bucket and a scrubbing brush, or a garden hose if you can. Try not to leave any paint particles on the brick surface. When all is dry, give the brickwork a scrub with a dry brush.

Pointing in the right direction

SIMPLE BRICK REPOINTING

The shaping of the mortar joints between bricks is known as pointing. Over time these joints can crumble and become porous, allowing water to penetrate the brickwork, which in turn can give rise to dampness that can freeze in cold conditions and cause further damage. You can undertake a small repointing task yourself. Doing the whole house is a job for the pros!

1 Rake out all the old and damaged mortar. Place the point of a plugging chisel on the mortar and tap it with a sledgehammer. Remember to wear gloves and goggles when you do this. Brush away any small particles with a stiff household brush.

need
* plugging chisel
* sledgehammer
* gloves and goggles
* stiff brush
* trowel
* prepackaged dry-mix mortar
* water
* mortar board
* Frenchman

TIP
Don't overwater the mortar mixture, because this can weaken it. It needs to be wet enough to be workable, but not sloppy.

2 Mix a small amount of mortar on a mortar board (or a sheet of stiff, flat board). Place a small heap of dry mortar in the middle of the board and make a well in the center. Pour a little cold water into the well and mix with the trowel. Add water little by little until the mortar reaches a workable consistency.

Don't start pointing if it looks like it's going to rain; you'll get wet and the mortar will be slow to set!

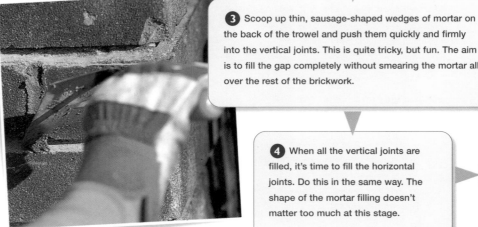

3 Scoop up thin, sausage-shaped wedges of mortar on the back of the trowel and push them quickly and firmly into the vertical joints. This is quite tricky, but fun. The aim is to fill the gap completely without smearing the mortar all over the rest of the brickwork.

4 When all the vertical joints are filled, it's time to fill the horizontal joints. Do this in the same way. The shape of the mortar filling doesn't matter too much at this stage.

MORTAR JOINT SHAPES

There are different ways to finish mortar joints. A flush joint is rubbed with a stiff brush to bring out the sand aggregate in the mortar. A raked joint emphasizes the bonding pattern of a wall and is achieved by scraping out the mortar with a thin wooden lath. This is not suitable for walls that are exposed to heavy weather. A rubbed joint is concave in profile; simply run a small piece of pipe along the mortar joint to create the shape, or use a mortar shaper. The sloping shape of weatherstruck joints directs water downward and away from the wall.

FLUSH JOINT

RAKED JOINT

RUBBED JOINT

WEATHERSTRUCK JOINTS

5 Use the point of the trowel to shape the mortar joints (*see above*). Do the verticals first, then the horizontals. Slide the trowel along the joints from top to bottom on the verticals and along each horizontal in turn.

6 Use your Frenchman to scoop up the bits of mortar that have been squeezed out by the pointing process. It is important to do this quickly because the mortar soon dries, and then you'll have a problem removing it. Hold the mortar board or trowel under the work area to catch falling blobs of mortar.

MAKING A FRENCHMAN

☞ C'est magnifique! The Frenchman is a very nifty tool for scraping excess mortar away from joints when a pointing job is complete (*see left*). You can make one easily by heating the blade of an old kitchen knife in the flame of a blowtorch or gas stove; when it's hot and malleable, bend the knife at right angles using a pair of pliers. Alternatively, you can make one from a strip of thin metal such as aluminum. The strip needs to be approximately 8 in. x 1 in. Bend the end at right angles again, then bind a portion of the straight part with masking tape to make a handle.

Frenchman

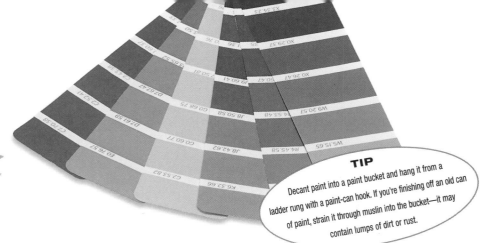

Now for the fun part—choosing color

PRIMING AND PAINTING EXTERIOR WALLS

24

So you've decided to paint your exterior because you fancy a new color or the old paint finish is looking a bit sad? Make sure that you have a few days in which to complete the task. Ideally the weather should be dry and warm but overcast. Masonry paint can be smooth or textured; simply decide which you prefer. Here comes the hard part—the color! Grab some color charts and take your pick. Just remember that you must use exterior-grade masonry paint: interior paint won't do (although the color range is better…).

need

* **extension ladder**
* **stiff brush**
* **fungicide**
* **exterior surface stabilizer**
* **exterior paint**
* **4-in. or 6-in. paintbrush**
* **narrow paintbrush**
* **gloves and goggles**
* **bucket and sponge**
* **paint bucket**
* **drop cloths**
* **newspaper**
* **masking tape**
* **mask**

safety is of the utmost importance (*see page 19*). Always make sure that the foot of the ladder is secured to the ground and that it leans against the wall at a safe angle, ideally about 70 degrees. There should never be more than one person up the ladder at any one time, and while you're on it, don't stretch out sideways: if you can't reach comfortably, move the ladder.

CALCULATING PAINT QUANTITIES

In general, paints will have an indication of the coverage area on the can. Simply calculate the approximate surface area of your house (i.e., multiply the height by the width of all the sides to be painted, then add all the figures together) and divide by the amount on the can.

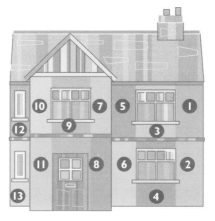

Masonry paintbrush

TIP

Decant paint into a paint bucket and hang it from a ladder rung with a paint-can hook. If you're finishing off an old can of paint, strain it through muslin into the bucket—it may contain lumps of dirt or rust.

ORDER OF WORK

☞ It pays to have a good plan of action when starting a big paint job like the front of a house. Use the numbered diagram above as a guide. Always apply paint to complete sections in turn, never stop painting halfway across a large area because this will show when the paint is dry. Use downspouts as natural breaks, so that you aren't left with obvious stop-start lines. Cover the ground with drop cloths to protect it from paint splashes and falling paint buckets or cans. Paint the walls first, then paint the window frames and doors.

TIP
Try using a long-handled roller to reach areas from ground level.

1 Spend time preparing the walls before painting. Use a stiff household brush to remove flakes of old paint and dirt. If green moss or mold is a problem, clean the surfaces thoroughly and brush the affected area with fungicide. Leave it for twenty-four hours and then hose down the walls with clean water. Allow them to dry completely before painting.

2 While the walls are drying, prepare the surrounding area by covering it with drop cloths. Take some sheets of newspaper and wrap them around all the downspouts, holding them in place with strips of masking tape. This takes all the stress out of painting behind them; simply remove the paper when the painting is completed.

* I ALWAYS LIKE TO DRESS FOR THE OCCASION!

3 Make any repairs—such as filling cracks—now and allow the filler to dry before continuing. If you find that the surface of the wall is chalky, apply a coat of a stabilizing primer. These products are usually colorless, but they are also available in white, which is quite an advantage if you're thinking of a color change. This one looks blue when wet but loses its color when dry.

4 Everything is now ready for painting. Use a large masonry paintbrush; if a stuccoed wall is highly textured, then you will need to use a stippling action, jabbing the brush against the surface to ensure good paint coverage. A roller can be used for smooth surfaces, but in general, rollers and paint trays are a bit of a nightmare when you're up a ladder. Use a narrower brush for awkward corners and when painting around door and window frames.

Repairing small cracks in walls

PATCHING EXTERIOR WALLS

Exterior walls are sometimes covered with layers of stucco, the surface of which can be smooth or slightly textured. The insulation properties of such an outer coating are clear, but you can be sure that small holes and cracks will form from time to time because of the weather. Any damage must be repaired as soon as you notice it—before things get out of hand and before any redecoration can be undertaken. Small cracks are easily repaired, but if you find that large chunks of stucco are falling off, then you should consider calling in a professional. Applying stucco to a large area is definitely not a job to do yourself.

need

* cold chisel
* short-handled sledgehammer
* trowel
* scraper
* stucco patching compound
* wall brush
* stiff brush

Laying it on with a trowel needn't make you look cheap!

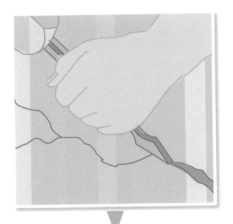

1 Rake out the crack in the surface of the stucco. Place the point of a cold chisel at the start of the crack and gently tap it with a sledgehammer to remove any loose or crumbling stucco—don't hack off big chunks. Brush away any dust with a large paintbrush.

2 Dampen the area surrounding the crack with some water: wet the bristles of a masonry brush and dab lightly. The stucco surface needs to be damp, not soaked— the dampness helps the filler adhere properly to the surface.

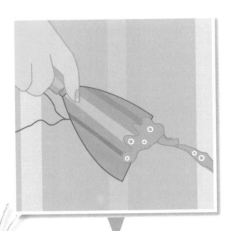

3 Use a scraper or trowel to fill the crack with patching compound. For long, thin cracks, fill with caulk from a caulk gun. To match a smooth-finished stucco, allow the patch to dry and rub it smooth with sandpaper.

4 If the surrounding surface is textured, apply a thinner layer of patch compound to the repair when it is dry and then use a stiff brush to texture it while it is still a bit soft. Repaint when completely dry.

PATCHING

CLAPBOARD AND WOOD LAP SIDING

26

☛ Clapboard, and other wood lap siding, consists of overlapping planks, or lap boards, that are nailed to the underlying sheathing. Because they overlap, rather than interlock, it is easy to replace a small damaged section.

need

* crowbar
* tenon saw
* chisel
* mini hacksaw
* try square
* pencil
* wooden shims
* hammer
* nails
* new piece of clapboard
* protective wood
* exterior wood caulk
* sandpaper

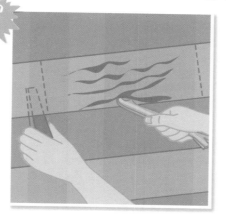

1 Mark lines on either side of the damaged area using a pencil, try square, and saw. The lines must be at right angles to the edge of the board. Use the crowbar to ease the damaged board out so that you can slide two shims underneath (just beyond the damaged area) to keep it raised.

2 Drive a thin piece of wood under the board where a saw line is marked. Use the tenon saw to cut along the line and a hammer and chisel to finish the cut, because it will be difficult to saw all the way through. Cut along the second line in the same way.

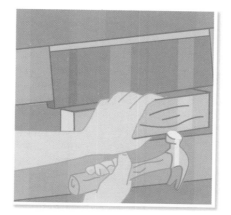

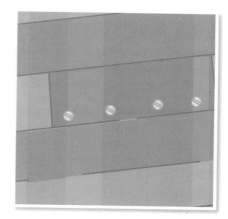

3 Remove the damaged part in one piece if you can, but if this is hard, then you may have to break it into pieces carefully. Old nails might also hinder your progress. If you find any passing through the board above, cut through them using a mini hacksaw. Slide the blade under the board, cut through the nail, and remove it as gently as possible.

4 Cut the new piece of board to fit the gap you have created. The fit will have to be exact, so measure across the top and the bottom of the gap just in case there are slight differences. Position the new piece between the cut ends of the old board, then place a spare length of wood along the lower edge and tap it home with a hammer.

5 When you are satisfied that the new piece fits perfectly you can nail or screw it securely in place. Fill the nail holes and joints at the ends of the board with an exterior-quality wood caulk and sand them smooth when they are dry. Apply a coat or two of paint so that the repair matches the rest of the siding.

Yes, it's time to use the power washer again!

CLEANING VINYL OR METAL SIDING

27

You have to admit that vinyl or metal siding is pretty tough, low-maintenance stuff. However, it's there on the outside of your house, exposed to the elements all year round, and you know what that means—dirt! Eventually it will require a good cleaning. It's best to do this job regularly to keep the exterior looking good.

USING THE POWER WASHER

Hey, it's the wonderful power washer again! This cool machine is just the ticket for cleaning siding. The water jet reaches all the nooks, crannies, and convoluted surfaces in which dirt and residue can collect. Don't do this on a very windy day because the water will just blow everywhere. Remember to wear rubber boots and rubber gloves, as this is a pretty wet job.

OPERATING INSTRUCTIONS

Do you keep instruction manuals for all your tools and equipment in a safe place? I do. This is not obsessive behavior; it makes good sense if you use a piece of equipment frequently (and if you have a power washer then you certainly will). Refer to the manual for full connection and operating instructions and maintenance procedures.

CLEANING BY HAND

Oh, dear! No power washer? Use a nice soft cloth and a big bucket of soapy water. This method is a little more time-consuming but it does the job eventually. It is most important not to use a brush or any kind of abrasive on metal or vinyl siding because this can scratch the surface.

need

* power washer
* rubber gloves
* rubber boots
* bucket
* cloth

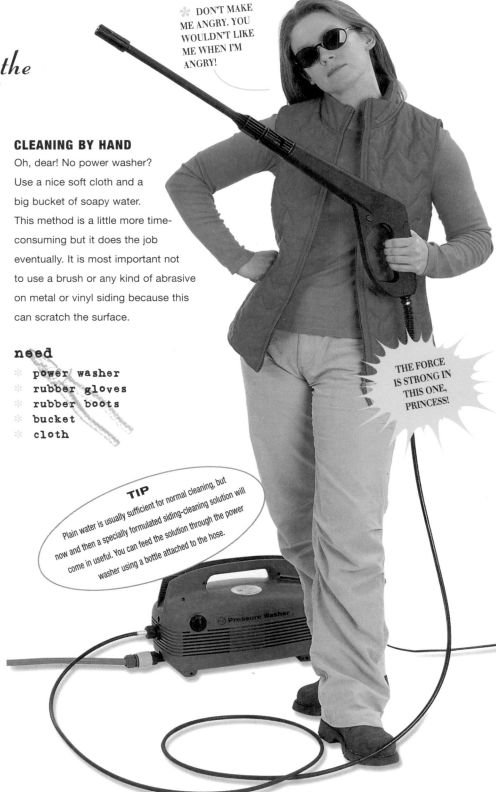

* DON'T MAKE ME ANGRY. YOU WOULDN'T LIKE ME WHEN I'M ANGRY!

THE FORCE IS STRONG IN THIS ONE, PRINCESS!

TIP
Plain water is usually sufficient for normal cleaning, but now and then a specially formulated siding-cleaning solution will come in useful. You can feed the solution through the power washer using a bottle attached to the hose.

REPAINTING WOOD LAP SIDING

Occasionally, a portion of your wood lap siding will rot or sustain damage. The only remedy is to remove it and replace it with a matching piece (*see page 75*). Small areas of damage, such as holes, can be repaired easily with an epoxy wood filler. Simply apply the filler, allow it to dry, sand smooth, and repaint. When a wooden siding board splits, it is not always necessary to remove the damaged part and replace it. Try this easy repair.

need

* waterproof wood glue
* chisel
* hammer
* nails
* cloth

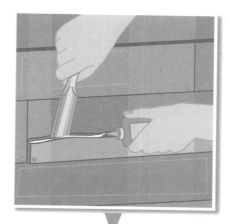

1 Locate the split board and place the chisel blade gently inside the split at the end of the board. Carefully hold the crack open (you can use a thin wooden shim for this) while you squeeze some wood glue into it, covering both sides liberally.

2 Allow the wood to spring back into the original position. Press the glued edges together tightly and secure the board to the sheathing underneath with finishing nails or screws. Use a damp cloth to wipe away any excess glue.

TYPES OF WOOD SIDING

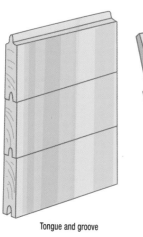
Tongue and groove

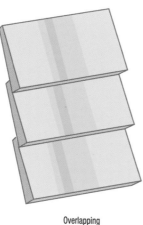
Overlapping

☞ Wood siding is available in many different profiles including overlapping (wood shingles and shakes, wood lap), tongue and groove, hardboard panels, and board and batten. Overlapping boards are nailed to studs or sheathing underneath and can be removed individually. Tongue-and-groove boards are interlocked, so removing them is more difficult. The damaged board must be cut across and lengthwise to facilitate removal. To repair board and batten siding, pry up the battens on either side of the damaged board. Then, raise and pull out the nail heads to remove the damaged portion.

WHEN PAINTING WOODEN SIDING, BEGIN AT THE TOP AND WORK DOWNWARD.

Keeping your walls and brickwork watertight

29

APPLYING SEALANTS AND WATERPROOFING

Sealants can be applied to just about any surface you can imagine in order to repel moisture, dirt, oil, and grease. In addition, caulking compounds can be used to weatherproof joints between adjacent surfaces. Check out all the fabulous products that are available these days. There's only one golden rule: clean the surface thoroughly first! There's no point in applying a sealant to a dirty surface because you'll just seal the dirt in, which is not a good idea. Weatherproof and seal garage floors, driveway walls, flat roofs, window frames, patios, exterior wood, furniture…you name it. Most sealant products are liquid, dry with a clear finish, and can be applied easily with a brush or roller.

TIP

Exterior woodwork or furniture can be sealed in the same way.

WALLS AND BRICKWORK

1 First, clean the surface to be treated, whether it's brick, concrete, or stucco. Use a wire brush to remove dirt and any loose particles. This will be a dusty job so be sure to wear a dust mask. If fungal growth is a problem on your brickwork or walls, apply a coat of good fungicide following the manufacturer's instructions. Fungicide can be applied with a brush and roller.

need

* **water sealant product**
* **rubber gloves**
* **wire brush**
* **trowel**
* **mortar**
* **large paintbrush**
* **paint bucket**

2 Repair any damaged areas. Repoint worn or crumbling joints with a trowel as shown and fill any cracks or holes with a suitable filler. Allow all repairs to dry completely before applying sealant.

3 Decant the sealant liquid into a small paint bucket so that it's easier to handle. If you're using a ladder, hang the bucket from one of the top rungs, leaving you with both hands free. Apply the sealant using a large brush, working from the bottom up. If the product requires a second coat, then allow adequate drying time before reapplication. Sealants are toxic, so keep the bucket and brush out of harm's way while you wait for the first application to dry.

SAFETY

☞ If using liquid sealants indoors—for example, on a garage floor—make sure that the area is adequately ventilated. The fumes given off by the sealant can be unpleasant and sometimes toxic.

☞ Wear rubber gloves; do not allow sealant products to come into contact with your skin.

☞ Wear a dust mask as an added precaution to prevent the inhalation of toxic fumes.

WINDOW FRAMES

need

* exterior-grade caulk cartridge
* caulking gun
* snap-blade knife

1 Insert the caulk cartridge into the gun and cut off the end of the nozzle with a snap-blade knife. Place the nozzle against the edge of the window frame. Press the trigger to release a thin, toothpaste-like bead of caulk.

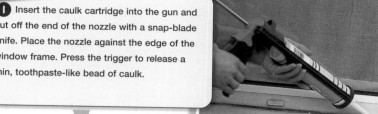

2 Run the caulking gun along all four sides of the window frame in order to create a sound, watertight seal. Most caulks set quite quickly and can be painted within a few hours. The beauty of caulk is that it doesn't set hard, it remains flexible. Remember to clean the frame and surrounding surfaces before sealing.

Caulking guns are great for sealing small gaps.

* I USUALLY STORE MY SEALANT GUN ON THE LEFT!

PATIOS AND PATHS

☞ Exterior floors like patios are subject to dirty feet, barbecue leftovers, and mold, as well as adverse weather conditions. Driveways and garage floors have oil spills and drips to contend with. Follow these easy steps and you'll have a pristine patio in no time.

1 Brush away loose debris, then use a patio cleaner with the same brush to remove dirt and fungus. Scrub the surface briskly and leave it for about ten minutes. Hose it down with clean water and let dry.

BLOCK PAVERS

2 Block paver sealant products are designed to penetrate deep into the surface of the blocks, drying with a highly durable, clear finish. The result is a surface that repels water, stains, oil, and grease, and is resistant to fungal growth, too. Apply two coats using a long-handled roller, allowing at least four hours drying time in between coats.

PAVING SLABS

2 Paving slab patios can be sealed to give a waterproof, stain-resistant surface, which will also reduce weather damage. Clean as in step 1 and apply a coat of sealant using a long-handled roller. Apply a second coat after two hours. Use a quick-drying product to ensure that the patio is ready for use in the minimum time.

need

* rubber boots
* rubber gloves
* floor brush
* bucket
* patio and paver cleaner
* hose
* patio sealer
* block paver sealer
* roller with long handle
* roller tray

Simple repairs for cracked or broken windows

REPANING A WINDOW

30

From time to time, windowpanes will break or crack and will need to be replaced. This can be due to many things, from stray footballs to severe weather conditions. If you are able to unhinge or slide the window from the frame, then remove it and do the repair indoors; if not, do it with the window in place. While it's a fairly simple matter to replace a small or medium-sized pane, anything larger than about 3 ft. should be left to a professional glazier. Glass is dangerous to handle at the best of times, so it's best not to risk having an accident with a large pane.

① First, with gloved hands, remove any pieces of broken glass. Then, using a chisel and the side of a hammer, remove all the putty. Put the blade of the chisel on the putty and gently tap the handle. If the putty is really old and hard, try softening it up with a blast from a heat gun. With a bit of luck, you will be able to scrape the putty away with a knife.

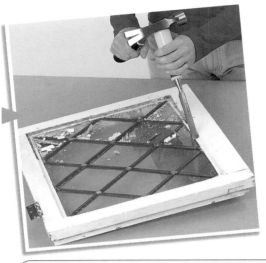

② When the putty has been removed, you'll probably see a few triangular or M-shaped glazier's points protruding from the frame. These are used to hold the glass pane in place. Pull them out carefully using long-nose pliers. Make sure the rabbet (the recess along the edge of the frame) is clean and smooth; sand it if necessary.

③ Take a small amount of putty in your hand and roll it into a really skinny sausage. Place the putty sausage into the corner of the rabbet all around. This creates a watertight seal between the glass and the frame.

※ MY, HER WINDOWS ARE ALMOST AS BRIGHT AND SHINY AS OUR TEETH!

※ LET'S HOPE THEY ARE FIXED IN AS FIRMLY!

4 Cut an 8-in. strip of duct tape and pinch the center together a bit to make a T-shape. Attach the sticky parts to the center of the glass. Pick up the glass with gloved hands and place it into the frame. Use the tape "handle" to ease it into position.

5 Use the chisel or putty knife to tap glazier's points into the rabbet all around to hold the pane in place. Take some more putty and roll it into a fatter sausage, about ½ in. in diameter. Squeeze small lumps of putty from the sausage all around the four sides of the pane using your forefinger.

need

* gloves and safety goggles
* new pane cut to size by glazier
* hammer and chisel
* heat gun
* long-nose pliers
* glazier's points
* duct tape
* putty
* angled putty knife

Wipe off stray putty while it's wet or it'll stick to the glass.

WASHING WINDOWS

 31

☞ Use a small paintbrush to clear dirt from the corners of the window frames. Fill the bucket with soapy water and get to work with a cloth or sponge. Rinse with clean water using a chamois leather cloth or even a sheet of scrunched-up newspaper (the grease in the printing ink makes the glass shine). You want the easy option? Give the windows a blast with the power washer and have some fun at the same time!

6 Use the putty knife to smooth out the putty; it has a forty-five-degree-angled part specifically designed for this purpose. Allow the putty to dry, then prime and repaint the window to match the others. Don't paint over damp putty—the paint finish will be ruined.

Learn how to be
a screen queen

MENDING SCREEN DOORS AND WINDOWS

32

Screening, whether aluminum or fiberglass, is not indestructible. Small tears in both types can be mended by dabbing a little silicone glue onto the tear. Aluminum screening can be "darned"; just unravel a few strands from a spare piece of mesh and use a needle to weave them over the tear. Both types can be patched: use glue for fiberglass or premade repair patches for aluminum. These have prehooked edges that clip onto the surrounding mesh. If the screen has sustained damage in several areas, then it's best to replace the screen completely— just follow the steps opposite.

Utility knife

SCREEN DOORS COME IN A VARIETY OF DECORATIVE YET FUNCTIONAL STYLES— AND SMALL REPAIRS ARE VERY EASY.

need

* screwdriver
* utility knife
* aluminum or fiberglass screening
* splining tool
* new spline

* I CHOSE FIBERGLASS AND LOOK AT ALL THIS MONEY I HAVE TO SPEND ON REAL SHOPPING!

Aluminum is more durable, but fiberglass is cheap and easier to install.

SPLINING TOOL

☞ You cannot replace a screen panel without a screen-installation splining tool! It looks very much like a double-ended pastry cutter with a wheel at each end. One wheel has a convex edge and is used for pushing the edge of the screening into the groove; the other wheel has a concave edge and is used to insert the rubber spline into the groove (it's the ropelike spline that keeps the screening in place). Spline tools come in two sizes, so be sure to choose one that fits the groove you have in your screen. Remember, use the right tool for the right job!

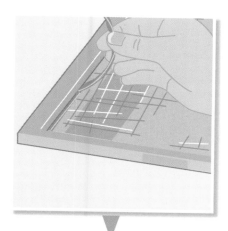

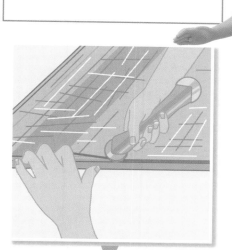

TIP

For aluminum screening, cut the new panel so it overlaps the frame by ½ in. Use the concave end of the tool to insert the spline and push the mesh into the groove at the same time. Trim excess away with a utility knife.

 I'M READY FOR MY CLOSE-UP NOW, MR. DEMILLE!

❶ Remove the old rubber spline and damaged screening. Ease the spline out of the groove with a screwdriver or the point of an awl. If you're careful you may be able to reuse the old spline for the replacement.

❷ Wipe the groove clean. Lay the screening on the frame and cut it to size with a utility knife. The edges should overlap the groove by ½ in. Cut across each corner diagonally, just inside the outer edge of the groove.

❸ Use the convex roller of the spline tool to push the edge of the screening into the spline groove. Position the roller at a forty-five-degree angle to the inside edge of the spline groove, and hold the screen taut while you work.

❹ Use the concave end to push the spline into the groove. Negotiate corners by bending the spline at right angles—do not cut the spline. When all sides are secured, use a utility knife to trim off excess screening.

Shut up and get on with it, girl!

ATTACHING DECORATIVE SHUTTERS

Exterior shutters can be decorative or functional; many people use them to emphasize or complement the architectural style of their homes. Traditional shutters are made of wood, which needs quite a lot of maintenance; repainting lots of shutters is a time-consuming task. Modern shutters are usually made from molded plastic, which is easy to care for, saving you time and effort. Decorative shutters are simply mounted on brackets attached to the exterior wall, so removal is easy when it's time for spring cleaning.

need

* shutters
* drill with hammer action
* awl
* screwdriver
* bracket or plastic fasteners
* hammer

* I NEVER KNEW SHUTTERS COULD BE SO CHIC!

INSTALLATION

☞ Fully operational shutters are supposed to cover the window completely to protect the glass and keep out drafts. Bear this in mind when you choose the size of your decorative shutters. Even if they don't actually work, they should at least appear to be the right size for the windows in order to look authentic.

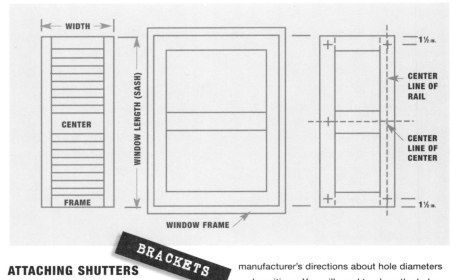

ATTACHING SHUTTERS — BRACKETS

1 Special shutter hardware is available to facilitate easy removal. Mark the desired shutter position on either side of the window.

2 Screw the brackets to the wall using the hardware provided. The shutter simply hangs on the bracket.

ATTACHING SHUTTERS — FASTENERS

1 Mark the shutter positions on either side of the window: make sure that they are level with each other. Drill screw holes through the shutter frame (most will not have predrilled holes): one on each corner and one at the center on both sides is usually sufficient. If you are attaching shutters to sidings, follow the manufacturer's directions about hole diameters and positions. You will need to place the holes at the highest point of the sidings to ensure that the shutter is fully supported.

2 Reposition the shutters against the wall, and using the drilled shutter as a template, mark the positions for the screw holes on the wall with an awl. Make a screw hole at each point, using a twist bit for wooden sidings and a masonry bit for brick or masonry.

3 The shutters are attached to the wall with plastic "Christmas tree" fasteners—the ribbed shafts are designed to better grip the wall. Gently tap each fastener in using your hammer. Be careful when using the hammer if the new shutters are made of molded plastic—one slip could cause damage to the shutter.

SOME SHUTTER STYLES

👉 Take your pick from the many shutter styles that are available. The shutters shown here would look fabulous both indoors and outdoors. Modern decorative shutters are sometimes molded from durable, maintenance-free vinyl. The colors are molded-through and are UV-stable, so there's no paint to chip, crack, or peel— simply install and admire!

Outdoor vinyl shutters require very little maintenance!

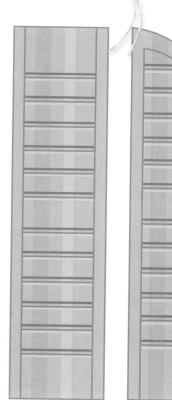

TIP
Most hardware stores and home centers will have a good selection to choose from, so do a bit of price checking before you buy.

Traditional style
✳ These outdoor shutters are molded in a traditional style with thin, open back or closed back louvers.

Plantation style
✳ The plantation-style shutters have wider louvers, which can be open back or closed back.

Raised panel style
✳ These are solid shutters with raised panels. All styles of shutters come with an option of quarter round arch tops.

Feel a storm brewing?

INSTALLING A STORM DOOR

34

A typical storm door has a glass pane or screen panel (or both) supported in a metal frame. In cold climates, a storm door will seal the main door against cold, while protecting the door itself from the elements. In warm weather, the glass panes can be replaced with screen panels so that you can open the main door without fear of bug invasion. Storm doors are easy to install; you just need to find a door to fit neatly around the opening of the existing door. Most units consist of a door with an integral mounting flange. It might also make sense to remove the glass panes, since this will make the unit lighter to handle during installation.

Drafty doors can be responsible for 40% of a building's energy losses.

need
* hammer
* drill
* screwdriver

HEY! MOUNTING A STORM DOOR

☞ First of all, choose which direction you'd like the door to open—that is, should the hinges be on the left or on the right? Screw the storm door's mounting flange directly to the existing frame. Predrill the screw holes first. Check that the door fits squarely within the door flange and seals tightly when closed. Attach door handles and locking mechanisms when the door is in position. The application of weatherstripping greatly reduces air leakage around the edge of the storm door.

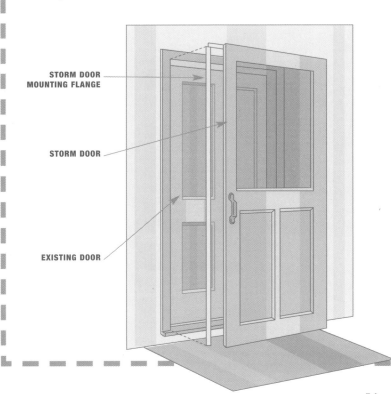

STORM DOOR MOUNTING FLANGE

STORM DOOR

EXISTING DOOR

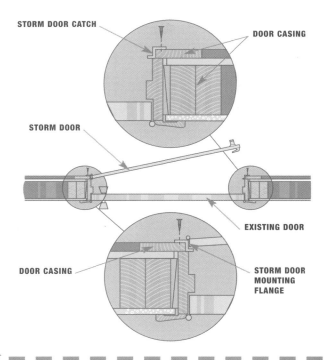

STORM DOOR CATCH

DOOR CASING

STORM DOOR

EXISTING DOOR

DOOR CASING

STORM DOOR MOUNTING FLANGE

INSTALLING STORM WINDOWS

Gone are the days when exterior shutters were used to protect windows from damage during storms—instead, try installing combination storm windows. Measure all your windows accurately and have the units custom-built to fit. Try each unit in its intended position and trim the edges a little with a tin snip to ensure a perfect fit. Aluminum storm windows usually have ribbed flanges to make trimming easy. Always trim off a little at a time and check the fit after each adjustment. You can always trim more off, but you can't put it back!

1 When you are satisfied with the fit of each unit, clean the window frame. Apply a bead of silicone caulk around the perimeter of the existing frame where the flanges of the new window will make contact.

2 Carefully lift each unit into position. Work around the perimeter, pressing the flange firmly so it makes contact with the caulk underneath. The caulk creates a watertight seal. Wipe away excess with a damp cloth.

ALL THE FUN OF THE STORM AND NONE OF THE MESS THANKS TO YOUR NEW STORM WINDOWS!

3 You can now screw your new combination storm windows securely to the existing window frames. Custom-built units will usually include screws with heads that match the flange, so the hardware will be as unobtrusive as possible

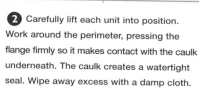

❋ QUIT MESSING WITH THOSE WINDOWS, LADY, AND COME HELP ME GET DRESSED!

need

* drill
* screwdriver
* tin snip
* caulking gun with exterior-grade caulk cartridge

Make a grand entrance

REPAINTING AN EXTERIOR DOOR

36

Exterior woodwork looks lovely when freshly painted, but every year Mother Nature sends a whole lot of lousy weather that doesn't bode well for paint finishes in the long term. I'm afraid, girls, that every few years you'll have to rub down and repaint the woodwork if you want your exterior to look great. Anyway, it's a good excuse to change the color, and that can't be bad, can it?

need

* sander
* dust mask
* screwdriver
* cloth
* bucket
* gloves
* exterior wood filler
* putty knife
* masking tape
* paintbrush
* primer, if wood is bare
* self-priming exterior enamel paint
* clear enamel exterior varnish

1 First, unscrew and remove the door handles and any other fittings. Remember to keep the spindle on your side of the door or you'll find yourself locked out if it slams shut! Wash all the woodwork and the threshold with soapy water to remove dirt and grease.

2 Examine the frame thoroughly for cracks in the wood or small imperfections in the surface. Using a putty knife with a flexible blade, fill all damaged areas so that they are flush with the surrounding timber. Wait until the filler has set completely. For large holes or deep cracks, apply the filler in thin layers, allowing each to dry before applying the next.

* WHAT GIRL DOESN'T APPRECIATE A GORGEOUS NEW COAT EVERY NOW AND THEN?

3 Use an electric sander to rub down all the surfaces until they are completely smooth, including the threshold. You could use sandpaper for this, but it really is hard work and I would recommend that you save yourself a bit of time and effort! Remember to wear a dust mask when sanding.

4 Mask off the edges of the glass panes with strips of masking tape. It is worth taking time to do this properly, because it protects the glass so you don't need to be so careful around the edges. Otherwise you'll be scraping the paint off the glass later.

YOU MAY COME ACROSS SOME OF THESE PROBLEMS!

WEATHER-SEAL MOLDING

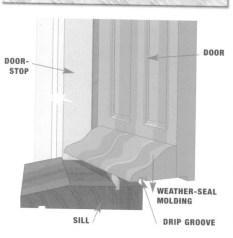

DOOR-STOP   DOOR

WEATHER-SEAL MOLDING

SILL   DRIP GROOVE

☞ Weather-seal molding is a molded strip of wood fitted across the bottom of an inward-opening external door. The aim of all sill weatherstripping is to make a weatherproof seal at the bottom of the door, deflecting rainwater away from the threshold underneath, and also to keep wind and rain from coming in through the door.

PAINT TROUBLE

☞ Peeling paint: the wood underneath is damp, dirty, or greasy, causing the top coat to lift, or the top coat was applied over flaky paint.

☞ Wrinkling paint: the top coat was applied too thickly, causing it to sag. Two thin coats are much better than one thick one.

☞ Cracking paint: a network of cracks appears if the top coat is applied before the undercoat is dry, or if the two coats are incompatible.

☞ Blistering paint: usually caused by trapped solvent vapor underneath the skin of paint, or moisture escaping from the wood. Sometimes blistering can be caused by exposure to strong sunlight, resulting in large, unsightly paint bubbles.

5 Stir the paint well before application. I used a self-priming exterior enamel paint suitable for wood or metal. This is a wonderful time-saver because there's no need to prime. However, if the wood is completely bare, I would advise that you prime first.

6 Now for the threshold. This is a piece of wood that is permanently fixed across the entrance to the door and which acts as a weather barrier (and trips you up occasionally if you forget it's there). Apply one or two coats of an exterior-quality, clear enamel varnish to seal and waterproof the wood, allowing the necessary drying time between applications. Pay special attention to the threshold because this gets the worst of the rain.

Rejuvenate your window frames

RENOVATING AND REPAINTING VINYL WINDOWS

37

Vinyl windows are relatively low maintenance. No wooden frame to rot, warp, or take care of, and they're double-glazed, too. However, plastic doesn't stay clean forever. So what's the answer? Manufacturers have now come up with specially formulated products that stick to plastic window frames. They are nonyellowing and contain fungicides to protect against mold. So you can now return your windows to their former glory and in any color, too!

These paints are low in volatile organic compounds, so they're not so bad for the environment.

1 Clean the window frame with warm soapy water or a special vinyl cleaner—the adhesion of the product relies on a spotlessly clean surface. Do not use a scrubbing brush or any abrasive because this will scratch the surface.

2 When the cleaning is done, take some time to mask off the edges of the glass on all four sides of each unit using strips of masking tape. This just makes your job a bit easier: the tape protects the glass from the paint so that you don't have to be so careful when painting around the edges. Peel off the tape when the painting is complete.

3 Stir the paint well and apply one even coat of vinyl gloss enamel (or primer if changing color). Use a synthetic brush suitable for water-based paint for the best results. Recoat after eight hours for gloss and four for primer.

4 When the first coat of paint or primer is dry, sand off any imperfections with a fine sandpaper and wipe away dust using a damp cloth. Apply the top coat of white or the first coat of colored gloss enamel paint and allow to dry. If you've taken the colorful option, you will probably need to apply another coat when the first is dry. Now clean your brushes with soapy water.

need
* vinyl cleaner
* soft cloth
* rubber gloves
* masking tape
* paintbrush
* sandpaper
* vinyl primer (if changing color)
* vinyl brilliant white gloss enamel (or exterior gloss enamel in a color)

TAKING CARE OF YOUR DOOR HARDWARE

38

Dull or corroded door hardware is not attractive; everybody wants their knobs, knockers, and handles to be nice and shiny. Metal fittings inevitably lose their shine after a while, but this can be remedied easily with a little metal polish, a soft cloth, and some good old-fashioned elbow grease. If the elements have taken a severe toll on your brass door fittings, you could find yourself with an ugly brown buildup of deposits that is difficult to polish away. Take one cup of hot water, add one tablespoon each of salt and vinegar, and apply the solution liberally to the affected item using a pad of fine steel wool. This will soften the deposits nicely; just rinse them with water, dry, and polish.

1 Put on your rubber gloves and mix up the solution in a small container. Take a short length of fine steel wool and roll it into a small pad. Apply the solution liberally to the brass fitting, working it into the surface with small circular movements. If possible, unscrew the fittings and do this on a table. If this is too difficult, do it with the fittings in place.

2 After a little while, you will see the nasty deposits dissolving before your eyes. When the brass looks clean, wash it with warm soapy water and rinse thoroughly with clean water. Dry it with a clean cloth.

* AND WHEN YOU'VE FINISHED THAT, YOU CAN BUFF UP MY SHINY NEW BOOTS!

3 Now put your back into it, girls. Polish the brass, using a lot of elbow grease, a soft cloth, and a little metal polish. It really doesn't take that long to do and the difference is remarkable. Better than buying new ones!

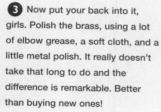

need

* rubber gloves
* plastic basin
* fine steel wool
* soft cloth
* salt
* vinegar
* metal polish

TIP

If you have brass numbers on your door, unscrew and submerge them in the salt-and-vinegar solution for a while before drying and polishing.

Keep railings looking gorgeous

RENOVATING CAST-IRON RAILINGS

39

Cast-iron railings are a wonderful feature, unless they're dirty and in need of a bit of cosmetic attention. Follow these simple steps to renovate any kind of exterior metalwork, including cast-iron downspouts, gates, and all sorts of decorative metal structures. Check your hardware store or home center for special metal paints and primers for galvanized steel and aluminum surfaces. Paint manufacturers are developing great new products all the time.

1 Put on a dust mask before you begin. Use the wire brush to remove loose paint flakes, rust particles, and any fungal growths. Brush in all directions so that you don't miss any intricate or convoluted areas. Be extra careful when cleaning paintwork that dates back to 1960 or earlier, because it may contain harmful lead. It is a good idea to do a job like this on a day with little or no wind—otherwise the paint particles and dust will blow everywhere.

2 Sand all surfaces with coarse sandpaper, taking the shine off the previous paintwork and creating a good base for the primer and top coats. Roll the sandpaper into a small tube to get into small, tight, or curved areas. Use a flexible sanding pad on intricately patterned surfaces.

 I JUST LOVE SHINY THINGS, DON'T YOU?

3 Use a specially formulated metal cleaner/degreaser to clean the railings thoroughly. Metal can be a tricky surface to paint on, so make it as easy on yourself as possible. Simply spray the cleaning product onto all the surfaces.

need

* rubber gloves
* dust mask
* paintbrushes
* bucket
* exterior metal primer
* exterior metal paint
* mineral spirits for cleaning up
* sandpaper
* wire brush
* cloth
* metal cleaner/ degreaser
* antirust product

4 Fill the bucket with warm soapy water. Wash the railings down to remove all residues and allow to dry completely. If you've discovered rust patches, apply an antirust product to the affected area and allow it to dry. Follow the directions on the product package; application with a small brush will usually suffice. It's just as important to treat small areas because rust will spread.

5 Using a clean brush, apply a liberal coat of primer and allow it to dry. If you do not intend to change the color of the metal, you can skip this stage and move directly to the top coat. Do a job like this on a warm, dry day; in windy weather, dust particles can blow onto the wet surface—then you'll have to re-sand and repaint.

The color range for exterior paints is getting broader all the time.

TIP
Use plenty of old newspaper to protect the surrounding area from drips.

6 Finally, when the primer is dry, apply one or two coats of paint. Always allow the necessary drying time between paint applications. If you are changing the color, two coats are advisable. In this case it is best to apply the paint in thick coats to provide a protective layer.

✻ MARRY ME, ALICE, AND WE CAN PAINT BEAUTIFUL RAILINGS TOGETHER!

DON'T FORGET TO TAKE THE CHAMPAGNE OUT FIRST!

Turning on the waterworks outside

INSTALLING AN OUTDOOR FAUCET

40

A faucet on an outside wall is a real advantage when it comes to pressure-washing exteriors or watering the garden. The only other alternative is to connect a garden hose to the cold water faucet at the kitchen sink, which can be tricky if the connector comes loose all the time, as mine used to! Outdoor faucet (hose-bib faucet) parts are available from hardware stores. You will need a self-cutting faucet with an integral double-check valve, a flexible hose with a protective sleeve, a brass, outside faucet with hose connector, and a brass wall plate.

PREPARATION

Before you start work, shut off the main water supply. Select a suitable position for the faucet; ideally, this should be within about 32 in. of the main water-supply pipe, after the rising main shutoff valve, and a suitable distance from the floor—that is, high enough to get a bucket underneath!

You can also buy cute decorative outdoor faucets in the shape of birds and animals!

Use a small pad of steel wool to clean the supply pipe where the inside faucet will be fitted. Unscrew the faucet body from the clamp and then remove both the slotted screws. Position the clamp around the pipe, making sure that the profiled sealing washer is in position. Insert and tighten the screws gently to grip the pipe.

Screw the self-cutting faucet into the clamp so that the cutter pierces the pipe wall. Adjust the faucet so that it is vertical and tighten the lock nut against the clamp. Attach the flexible hose to the faucet. Drill a 1-in. access hole through the wall from the inside. Pass the hose through the hole. Next follow the instructions opposite for installing the outdoor faucet.

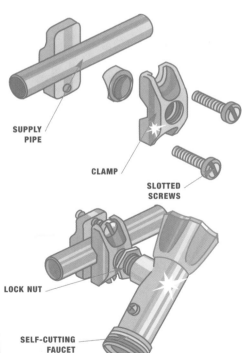

SUPPLY PIPE

CLAMP

SLOTTED SCREWS

LOCK NUT

SELF-CUTTING FAUCET

ANATOMY

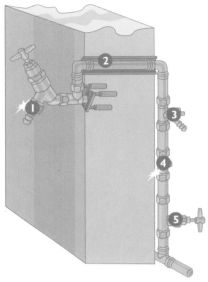

☛ Because the faucet is connected to the main supply, a double-seal, nonreturn valve must be fitted between the main pipe and the faucet. This keeps contaminated water from being drawn back into the main supply. If you intend to use a faucet installation kit, then the pipe-cutter faucet assembly also serves as the nonreturn valve. A flexible hose means you have no complicated pipe bends to create when running the supply through the wall.

❶ Angled bib faucet and threaded nozzle ❷ Length of plastic overflow tube ❸ Stop-and-waste valve ❹ Double-seal nonreturn valve ❺ Shutoff valve

WARNING

☛ Make sure there are no concealed pipes or cables in the wall before you start drilling.

1 Choose a suitable position for the wall plate on the outside wall. Hold the plate to the wall and mark each screw hole using the point of an awl. Using the smaller bit, drill a hole at each of the marker points, then insert wall anchors into each one. Screw the plate securely to the wall.

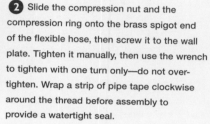

2 Slide the compression nut and the compression ring onto the brass spigot end of the flexible hose, then screw it to the wall plate. Tighten it manually, then use the wrench to tighten with one turn only—do not over-tighten. Wrap a strip of pipe tape clockwise around the thread before assembly to provide a watertight seal.

3 Attach the faucet to the wall plate to complete the job. Again, wrap a short strip of pipe tape clockwise around the thread to ensure a watertight seal.

4 To test, turn the main supply on and open the outside faucet to flush out any debris. Close the outside faucet and check all the seals for signs of leakage. You can now fill up your bucket with water!

need

* self-cutting faucet with integral double-check valve
* flexible hose with protective sleeve
* brass outdoor faucet with hose connector
* brass wall plate
* awl
* screwdriver
* wrench
* drill and ¾-in. diameter masonry bit
* ¼-in. diameter masonry bit
* steel wool
* all-purpose sealant
* pipe tape

OH STEVE, TURN OFF THE SHUTOFF VALVE BEFORE SOMETHING HAPPENS THAT WE'LL BOTH REGRET!

NOW THAT'S WHAT I CALL A TURN-ON!

Coming to grips with pipes

CUTTING PIPES

41

☞ Here's how you should deal with pipe-cutting. First, buy yourself a pipe cutter. This looks a lot like a C-clamp, but has a cutting wheel and an adjustable screw with small rollers on the end. It also has a little triangular blade that pulls out to deburr the cut edge of the pipe. This device will cut pipes at an exact ninety-degree angle every time.

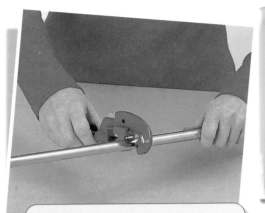

NO PIPE CUTTER?

☞ As an alternative to buying a pipe cutter, you can cut a pipe with a hacksaw. It's much harder work, but not too difficult. Wrap a strip of paper around the tube, matching up the straight edges, and attach it with a piece of masking tape. Cut through the pipe using the edge of the paper as a guide; this way the cut will be straight and at right angles to the pipe.

❶ Calculate the length of pipe needed and mark the pipe accordingly. Place the pipe in the cutter and align the circular blade with the cutting line. If the pipe is old or dirty, then clean the area to be cut using a small pad of steel wool. This will ensure that the blade makes a good cut.

need
* **length of pipe to cut**
* **pencil**
* **pipe cutter**

❷ Tighten the screw to hold the pipe firmly, then rotate the pipe slowly, tightening the screw a little after every revolution. The blade will cut cleanly through the metal after a few turns. Proceed slowly and do not be tempted to adjust the screw too quickly, because this may cause the pipe to dent.

❸ The action of the pipe cutter ensures a smooth edge on the outside of the pipe but not the inside. Snap open the deburring blade and insert it into the end of the pipe. Rotate the pipe against the tool, smoothing the rough edges and taking off all the burrs.

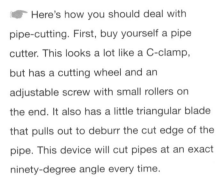

❋ NO WAY, HONEY! YOU'RE NOT CUTTING THIS PIPE!

Pipe cutter

REPAIRING AN OUTDOOR FAUCET

Basic faucet repairs are not difficult—all you need is a wrench and a firm grip. If the faucet leaks from the spout when in the closed position then you'll probably find that the rubber washer inside has worn out. A hose-bib faucet is a primitive beast; there's no special outer cover to remove, and the stem is exposed and is therefore quite easy to dismantle.

✳ DON'T WORRY, I'VE SNIPPED LOTS OF PIPES BEFORE!

1 Firmly grip the faucet handle and place the jaws of the wrench around the stem locknut. Adjust the wrench so that it grips the nut tightly. While maintaining your grip on the handle, rotate the wrench to loosen the nut. You may have to grit your teeth a bit while you do this, but it will eventually come loose!

need
✳ large, adjustable wrench
✳ screwdriver
✳ new washer

2 Unscrew the stem from the faucet casing. You will see a black rubber washer on a little button (or held in place by a screw) at the base of the assembly. Gently pry the washer off the button. Use a screwdriver if necessary. If the washer is held in place by a screw, unscrew it to remove the washer.

3 Replace the washer and reassemble the faucet. Just to make sure that all screw joints are watertight and sealed, wrap a little pipe tape around the thread before reassembly.

TIP
Dismantle the faucet, then remove the washer. Take the old one to the store with you to make sure the new one is the same size.

Lots more fun to be had with water in the garden

43

MENDING A HOSE

Do you have an old garden hose? A kind friend gave her old hose to me when I moved to my new home, and I was of course delighted to receive it. However, it soon sprang a leak, as old hoses tend to do. It is possible to attempt a makeshift repair with a bicycle repair kit or some adhesive tape, but why fudge it when you can just get a hose repair unit like this and do the job properly? I was amazed at the range of hose gadgets and attachments that are readily available these days. A hose repair connector is a wonderful device that can be used either to make repairs or join lengths together. Easy!

To make that sure your hose has a long and efficient life, follow the hose care instructions opposite.

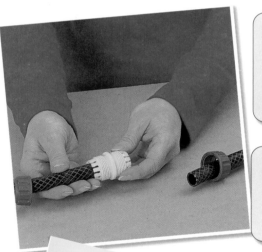

Water the garden and pot plants during the coolest part of the day to help minimize evaporation.

> **HOSE CARE**
>
> Always coil your hose neatly after use, or, better still, mount it on a reel so that it won't get tangled. Try not to leave a long hose trailing all over the garden for someone to trip over. Most hoses are green so that they are almost invisible in the grass. Make sure that your hose has no kinks in it, because these can hinder water flow. If the hose doesn't work when you try to use it, on no account look down the end to see what's wrong—you could get a jet of water right in your eye.

1 Cut out the damaged section of the hose using a utility knife. Unscrew both plastic ends of the connector, exposing the central part of the unit. Slip one of the ends onto each piece of hose, making sure that the thread faces the cut end. Now push the hose ends into the grips of the central unit.

2 Make sure that both ends of the hose fit snugly in the central unit, then screw on the end parts tightly. This action causes the prongs of the plastic grip to squeeze the hose, thus making a good watertight seal. Because this process doesn't involve glue, you can undo the connection at any time—perhaps to add a longer section of hose.

need
* utility knife
* hose repair connector

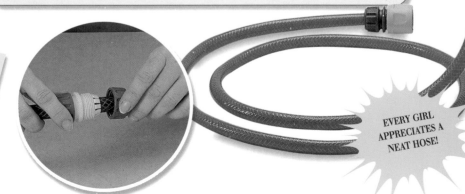

EVERY GIRL APPRECIATES A NEAT HOSE!

MAINTAINING A SPRINKLER SYSTEM

An in-ground sprinkler system is a wonderful labor-saving device, particularly if you have a large lawn or if you're an avid gardener with vegetable patches and other areas that need regular irrigation. Check the sprinkler heads from time to time to see that they're not clogged with dirt or mineral deposits. If you spring a leak, then you'll need to dig down to the pipe and repair it. This will make you wish that the previous owner had left you the sprinkler pipe plan.

❋ ADJUST THE UMBRELLA, SON, YOUR MOTHER'S TESTING THE SPRINKLER AGAIN!

POSITIONING A SPRINKLER

First, think about your dimensions. Make a scaled-down plan of the lawn, planting areas, walkways, and so on. Take this along when you buy the essential components. It will be of use to you and the salesperson. Sprinkler systems are available in kit form and are easily installed. A typical kit includes all the pieces you need: sprinkler heads, an antisyphon valve, a timer, and lots of PVC pipe. Garden centers are bristling with new systems that are easy to install, so shop around. Read all the instructions thoroughly before starting work. The diagram shows a typical sprinkler system with underground pipes, sprinklers, and a timer control.

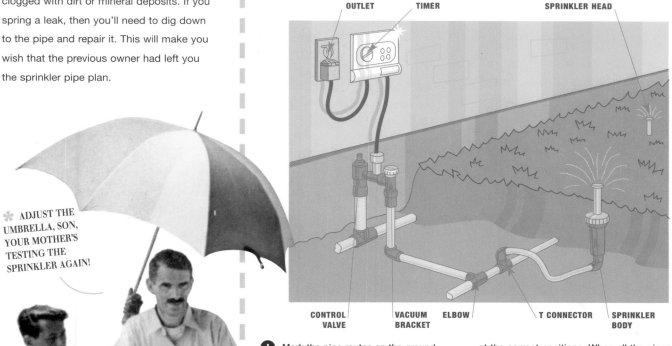

OUTDOOR OUTLET   TIMER   SPRINKLER HEAD

CONTROL VALVE   VACUUM BRACKET   ELBOW   T CONNECTOR   SPRINKLER BODY

① Mark the pipe routes on the ground surface using string or a series of pegs.

② Dig a narrow V-shaped trench of about 6–10 in. depth, depending on the length of the sprinkler heads, along the lines marked.

③ Roll out the PVC pipe along the trenches, placing sprinklers on the ground at the correct positions. When all the pipes have been laid, join up the sprinklers as indicated in the instructions, then replace the soil in the trenches.

④ Now that you've done most of the hard digging, get a plumber in to complete the job (i.e., fitting the antisyphon device, timer, and connection to the main water supply).

Simple steps to laundry heaven

PUTTING UP A CLOTHESLINE

46

On a warm, sunny, breezy day, there's something really satisfying about hanging your laundry out to dry. Clothes dried in the sunshine have a lovely fresh smell, too. My small apartment is definitely not suited to laundry, so I love the summer—I can peg everything on the line and my washing is dry in no time. Better than racks of damp laundry cluttering up your living space, and much better for your house guests, too!

1 Choose the position for the hook, then use your ladder to reach the area safely. Mark the hole position with chalk. Fit your drill with a big fat ½-in. masonry bit. You need a heavy-duty anchor for the heavy-duty hook; damp laundry can be really heavy and you don't want the hook to come out. Put on your safety goggles and drill the hole.

2 Blow into the screw hole to remove brick or masonry dust, then use a hammer to tap the wall anchor into the hole so that the rim is flush with the wall. The wall plug should fit snugly. It's a good idea to wear your tool belt so that you can carry all your equipment with you. Screw the hook into the wall.

3 Attach a cleat to the wall at a point directly below the hook at about shoulder height. Use this to secure the clothesline when it's raised to its highest position (like strings on a blind).

4 Hold the cleat up to the wall and mark the screw-hole positions. Swap the drill bit for a smaller one and drill the holes where indicated—don't forget to wear your goggles. Tap a wall anchor into each hole and screw the cleat into place.

5 You'll need the ladder again for this. Tie the clothesline to a sturdy tree if you have one; if you don't, buy a metal washing-line pole and set it in concrete just like a fence post (*see page 147*). Thread the other end of the line through the pulley and hang it from the hook. Pull the clothesline taut and secure the loose end around the cleat.

need

* ladder
* drill with a ½-in. masonry bit
* ½-in. wall anchor
* goggles
* hammer
* small masonry bit and matching anchors
* large hook
* pulley
* cleat
* clothesline
* line post

PUTTING IN A CAT FLAP

If you have a cat, it's a good idea to install a cat flap so that kitty can come and go as and when she pleases. Most kits contain full instructions, cutting templates, and hardware. They usually have locking mechanisms, too, so that you can keep the cat in or out when you need to. This is a basic, inexpensive model but there are lots of different ones, including those that are operated by sensors on the cat's collar. I found it easier to remove the door from the frame in order to mark and cut the hole on the workbench. You can do it with the door on the frame, but it makes it a bit more difficult to use the jigsaw.

need

* cat-flap kit
* pencil
* drill
* jigsaw with scrolling blade
* screwdriver

1 Take the door off its hinges and place it flat on your workbench. Remove the cat flap from the box, read the instructions, and check that you have all the hardware. Place the cutting template in position on the lower door panel; it needs to be in the center, at least 6 in. from the lower edge of the door. Draw around the template using the pencil. Lift up the edge of the template before removing it to check that the outline is clear.

TIP
Be careful when using the jigsaw—don't cut holes in your lovely workbench!

2 Use your drill to make pilot holes just inside both top corners of the outline. Insert the jigsaw blade in the top right-hand pilot hole and begin to cut as close to the pencil outline as you can. Proceed slowly and carefully. Remove the cut-out section and discard it.

3 The cat flap comes in two parts: the flap screws to the front of the door and the trim fits on the back with a self-adhesive strip.

4 Place the front part into the cut-out area, and screw it securely in place with the screws provided. Cover the screw heads with plastic caps. Attach the trim to the back. For a finishing touch you can paint the frame to match the door!

✳ SHE REALLY KNOWS HOW TO MAKE AN ENTRANCE!

Open sesame—garage door servicing

MAINTAINING GARAGE DOORS

48

Any mechanism or device with moving parts must be well maintained and lubricated if it is to operate efficiently in the long term. Garage doors are no exception and need regular attention to keep them in shape.

MAINTENANCE

You should clean and lubricate all the moving parts of your garage doors—roller bearings, pulleys, lock mechanisms, and cables—at least once a year to avoid problems and a sticky door. All you need to do is inspect every part of the mechanism and brush away any accumulated grease or dirt using a small brush. Once you've gotten rid of the grease and grime, put your gloves on and give everything a quick spray with a spray lubricant. Don't forget the lock mechanisms, because they can seize up and cause problems if neglected for a long time. Spray some lubricant into the keyhole, then work the key in and out a few times to make sure all is operating efficiently. If your doors are hinged and open outward, then simply oil the hinges. Check for loose hinges and brackets as well and tighten them where necessary.

AND TYPES OF GARAGE DOORS

Sectional overhead doors

✳ Sectional overhead doors are usually made from metal panels that hinge together and slide on a pair of tracks inside the garage. The door retracts when opened, which is useful if space is limited and it would be inconvenient for the doors to swing outward. Key areas to take care of on these doors are the tracks and the hinges between the door panels to ensure a smooth action.

Up-and-over doors

✳ Typical up-and-over-style doors are counterbalanced and slide on a pair of vertical tracks, one on each side of the doorway. The lower portion of the door swings outward, then slides upward and over into the garage. This type of door requires a certain amount of effort to open and close it, so you can see why it's important to keep all the moving parts well lubricated.

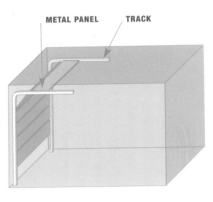

METAL PANEL   TRACK

DOOR SWINGS OUT THEN UP   TRACK

WARNING

☞ A word about fancy, electric, automatic garage door openers. Check that these have an automatic reversing mechanism, so that if the door meets with any resistance during the closing operation, it will reverse. This means that it won't close on you or your car. If it doesn't have this feature, it is potentially dangerous.

✳ FAULTY GARAGE DOORS? ALLOW ME AND MY TRUSTY CHOPPER TO HELP YOU OUT!

need
* small brush
* gloves
* spray lubricant

GARAGE DOOR MECHANISM

☞ Before installation can take place, a solid wood frame must be fitted securely around the doorway to give adequate clearance at the sides and the top and to provide firm attachment points for the mechanism. Some companies will include a frame with the door, and this will be included in the overall measurement. Automatic door opening mechanisms can be fitted to most sectional or up-and-over garage doors. These devices are electrically operated and make your life so much easier—no more hauling a heavy door up and down. Usually the door is opened remotely from inside or out using a handheld control. If you need to replace a garage door or opening mechanism, then this will be a job for a contractor—maintenance is the easy part.

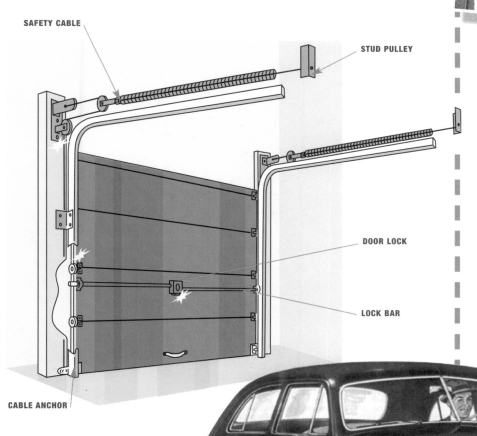

SAFETY CABLE

STUD PULLEY

DOOR LOCK

LOCK BAR

CABLE ANCHOR

THAWING FROZEN PIPES

49

Winter brings cold weather, and—if you're unlucky—frozen pipes. Prevention is better than cure so try to insulate vulnerable pipes, like those that run through attics, basements, or under floors. If the tank won't fill or a faucet refuses to work, this is a sure sign that water has frozen in one of the supply pipes. Outdoor faucets are prime targets for winter freeze-ups. Locate the problematic pipe and blow hot air from a hairdryer over the affected part. Copper pipes conduct heat quickly and the ice plug inside the pipe will melt, resulting in normal water flow. Leave the faucet open so you know when the problem has been solved.

✳ GREAT JOB ON THE DOORS, HONEY! HOW D'YA WORK THIS ROUND THING?

Water, water, everywhere...how to deal with floods and blockages

Or you could just call the fire brigade and watch them do it instead!

PUMPING OUT A BASEMENT

Crisis! You have a flood in your basement. If the flood was caused by a burst pipe, turn off the water supply by closing the main shutoff valve. Put on your rubber boots and rubber gloves and salvage anything of value. Think about how such an event can be avoided in the future: make sure that all pipes that run under floorboards, through basements, or in attic areas are properly insulated. I used to live in a house where the basement would fill with water from time to time—something to do with the water table, I was told. This kind

of periodic water-level rise is a nuisance. If you are unfortunate enough to have a problem like this on your hands, rent a submersible pump and hose. The rental store staff will show you how to use the equipment safely and efficiently. The pump is placed under the water and it pumps it out through the hose. You must make sure that the end of the pipe is placed near a main drain so that it runs off safely. When all the water has been pumped away, you can rent a big hot-air blower to dry the area out.

need
* **rubber boots**
* **rubber gloves**
* **submersible pump and hose**
* **hot-air blower**

Submersible pump and hose

AND

TACKLING DAMPNESS

☞ Dampness in basements may not be caused by flooding. Because the basement is underground, or partially underground, excessive condensation can form on the walls because they are colder than the air inside the basement. This kind of dampness can be treated by applying a specially formulated sealant to the walls and floors to create a barrier. To determine whether the dampness is seeping in/up from the surrounding ground or is the result of condensation, try a few elimination processes. Make sure that the basement is well ventilated and rent/buy a dehumidifier unit. Still damp? Check that all rainwater drainage systems are clear and functioning effectively; there might be a blocked downpipe overflowing next to the basement. Patios might have settled and dropped a little, directing water toward the house and basement. A nearby tree might be interfering with your foundations. If the source isn't obvious, call in the experts.

THIS YEAR'S ABSOLUTE MUST-HAVES!

UNBLOCKING MAIN DRAINS

51

Blocked drains are obviously pretty unpleasant, but sometimes there's no alternative to gritting your teeth and getting on with the task.

TAKE THE PLUNGE

If you have a blockage in a toilet that a plunger won't solve, try using a closet auger, a shorter version of a drain auger. If that doesn't work, the blockage could be in a branch drain below the affected toilet or in the main drain. For this you'll need to rent a drain auger or drain auger rods and attachments. Locate the cleanout fitting at the end of a branch drain or of the main drain and place a bucket under it. Shut off the main water supply and loosen the cleanout plug to release the backed-up water. Remove the plug and push the end of the auger cable into the drain. Crank the auger until it engages and dislodges the obstruction. Flush the pipe with fresh water from a hose and disinfect the whole area.

need

* rubber gloves
* drain auger rods
* drain auger attachments
* disinfectant

Plunger head

Drain auger attachments

These scary-looking torture instruments are drain auger attachments. You can rent a set to deal with the most stubborn of blockages (*see also page 20*). Just get your rubber gloves on, push the auger with desired attachment into the drain, then crank, push, and pull until the blockage clears.

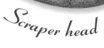

Corkscrew head

Scraper head

WE MAY LOOK STIFF, BUT WE CAN BEND TO FIT ANYWHERE!

✳ I ALWAYS MOISTURIZE AFTER A LONG, HARD SESSION WITH MY FLEXIBLE RODS!

Drain auger rods

These are flexible rods that join together, and they come with a selection of fittings to attach to the end—plungers, corkscrews, and scrapers (*see above*).

TIP

If all else fails, call in the pros.

Making a birdhouse

52

Now that you've completed all that exterior maintenance, why not get creative and make a pretty birdhouse to add a nice finishing touch to the yard? As we all know, birds have a hard time finding enough food during the winter months, so I'm sure they'll be very pleased to have a helping hand. Make sure that you place the birdhouse in a quiet spot so the birds will not be disturbed or frightened away by passersby. It's also good to place the birdhouse near a window so that you can watch the birds. Birds like bread, seeds, and nuts, and be sure to put a dish of fresh water out for them, too—they may drink it or even bathe in it!

need

* pencil and tracing paper
* pine board or old hardwood shelving
* 1¼-in. x ½-in. wooden cleats
* piece of plywood for the base
* wooden fence post
* metal fence-post spike
* sledgehammer
* four small brass right-angle brackets plus screws
* wooden plant markers
* fence boards
* jigsaw
* sandpaper
* saw
* hammer
* 1-in. nails
* screwdriver
* household scissors
* masking tape
* exterior gloss enamel
* paintbrush
* artist's paintbrush
* wood glue

1 To begin, trace the templates (*see page 182*), then redraw each one at full size. You will need a front, a back, and two sides. Cut out the paper templates and draw the outlines on the pine board. Use a jigsaw to cut out the shapes, then smooth off any rough edges using sandpaper.

2 Cut four 10-in.-long wooden cleats. These will be used to strengthen the walls of the birdhouse where they meet at each corner. Use wood glue to attach the cleats to the side pieces.

3 Press firmly into position to expel any excess glue, which should be wiped away before it dries. When the glue is dry, nail the cleats securely in place.

4 You now need to attach four cleats in place across the base of the archways on all four sides to support the shape (and to keep the bird food from falling out). At the front and back, cut, glue, and nail cleats to fit exactly across the arch.

5 For the sides, attach the cleats in the same way, but make them a little longer at each end to accommodate the width of the cleats on the front and back. When the sides are nailed together, the cleats form a little wall all around. Construct the house as shown in the diagram on page 182. Don't forget the stabilizing cleat at the peak.

6 Use your household scissors to cut the wood plant markers in half; you will need about twenty halves. Take two spare pieces of cleat and attach the ends of each half-marker to the cleats with pieces of masking tape. Paint half the markers pink and half of them blue on both sides.

7 Cut a piece of plywood to fit the base, then glue and nail it in place. Paint the birdhouse inside and out. When the paint is dry, use wood glue to stick the painted markers to the inside of the perimeter wall down both sides, just like a picket fence.

8 Cut six pieces of fence board, about 4 in. longer than the measurement across the roof from front to back. Paint six pieces pink and two blue. Nail the pieces in place on the roof, starting at the lower eaves and working up toward the peak, overlapping as you go. The boards should protrude by about 2 in. at the front and back and along the eaves.

9 To mount the birdhouse, first paint the fence post, then drive the metal fence-post spike into the ground. Place the fence post in the spike: you may have to help it a little with the sledgehammer (*see page 146, "Installing a panel fence"*). Attach it to the underside of the house using brass screws and right-angle brackets.

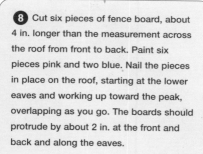

✱ HIGH-RISE LIVING? IT'S FOR THE BIRDS!

TIP
I've used some old hardwood shelves to make the sides of the birdhouse here, but pine board is just as good. Prime and paint it with exterior-quality paint to protect it.

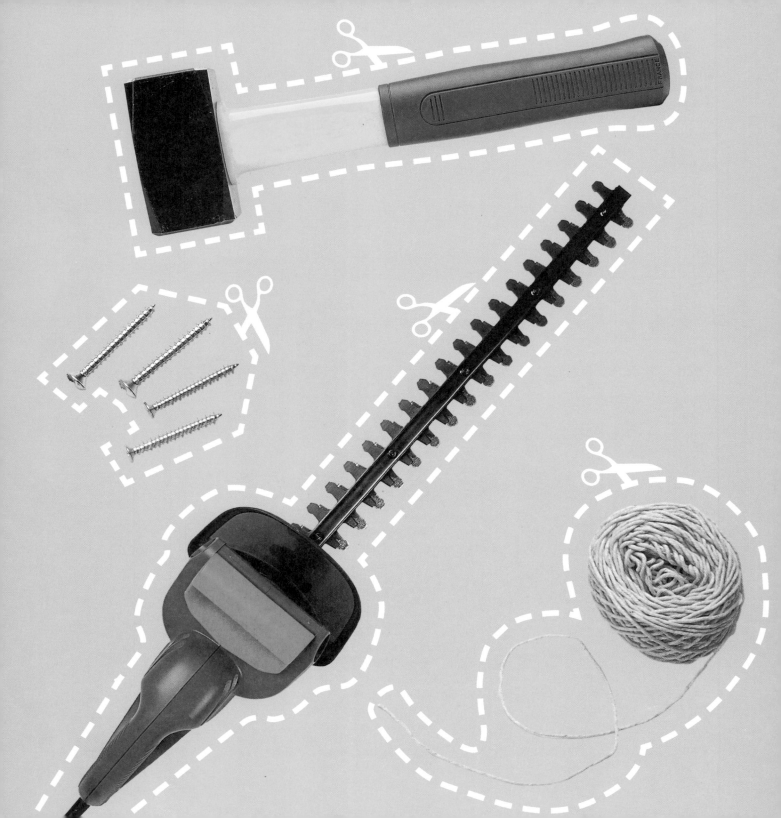

GETTING GROUNDED

Get your backyard back into great shape with lovely lawns, perfect patios, delightful decking, and so much more...

Making the backyard lovely

LET'S START at ground level, shall we? If you're lucky enough to have inherited a beautiful garden, then you should just feel very pleased with yourself, sit somewhere comfortable, and relax. But if, as in my case, your garden is a bit of a jungle (admittedly, mine got like that through sheer neglect—well, I was working on my apartment!), one of the first things you'll need to do in the garden is clear up.

CLEANING AND PAINTING A CONCRETE FLOOR

53

Concrete surfaces in garden areas and concrete floors in garages and basements tend to be magnets for dirt and grime. The textured surface captures dirt and oily stains and eventually looks rather worn. It might even become dangerous to walk on, especially in wet weather. Give the floor a really good cleaning, then apply a coat or two of heavy-duty floor paint to create an attractive antislip surface (most paints of this type contain antislip agents). You can choose a neutral color or go for a complete change. Pink concrete—just imagine!

TIP
Remove rust stains from concrete using bleach and a small, stiff brush.

1 Before using detergents or water, brush away surface debris and organic matter using a stiff brush. If there are any stubborn oil stains to remove, use a specially formulated cleaner worked undiluted into the stain with a small brush. Leave for the length of time specified by the manufacturer, then rinse with a solution of four parts water to one part cleaner, applied with a stiff brush.

2 If the concrete is not stained but simply grubby with ingrained dirt, a power washer should do the trick. Put on your rubber boots, connect the washer to a faucet with a garden hose, and away you go.

3 The water-jet dislodges stubborn dirt, leaving shiny, clean concrete; the difference in color is amazing. Allow to dry before applying any paint or sealer.

4 If the surface of the clean concrete is dusty or porous, apply a coat of sealer—this will help the top coat of paint go further. Decant the sealer into a shallow paint tray placed on the floor near your feet. Use a roller with an extending handle to save your back. When the sealer is dry, apply a coat or two of floor paint in the color of your choice, using a roller as before.

need

* stiff brush
* small hand brush
* cleaning product for driveways/patios
* bucket
* low-pressure power washer
* hose
* rubber gloves
* rubber boots
* long-handled roller
* paint tray
* heavy-duty floor paint
* sealer (optional)

BUSH CLEARING AND TRIMMING

54

When the time for jungle clearance arrives, wear rubber boots, put on your gloves, and resign yourself to hard work. It is best to do this in the fall when your plants are dying back. Work from the top downward: first, prune and trim trees, bushes, and large shrubs, then attack lower-lying plants. After that, get down in the dirt, turning over the topsoil along borders and removing any weeds and undesirables as you go. Last but not least, mow the grass!

1 Pruners are usually sufficient for general low, light undergrowth and bush clearance, but when you're faced with high or thick branches, a long-handled lopper is what you need. Simply snip off the offending branches.

2 Collect all the pruned and trimmed branches and any other woody organic matter, and set up your shredder in a level position. Feed the trimmings into the shredder and let it do all the hard work for you! Don't forget to place a large bag underneath the outlet to catch the shredded pieces. The resulting chippings make fabulous mulch to use along the borders of garden pathways.

※ YOU WILL NOT BELIEVE WHAT I'VE JUST SEEN!

need
* gloves
* rubber boots
* mower
* pruners
* lopper
* shredder
* leaf rake
* hand trowel and fork
* large bags to collect debris

SAVE LEAVES FOR THE COMPOST!

WARNING
☞ You will probably need to use an outdoor extension cord for the shredder, so remember to use a GFCI.

PRUNING AND LOPPING

Keeping small trees in shape is simple, and it will help them to stay healthy. All you need is a pruning saw, a pruning knife, and a little spare time.

☞ Using a pruning saw, make a cut about halfway through the branch on the underside, approximately 10 in. from the trunk.
☞ Now make a second cut close to the first, from the top downward, again about halfway through the branch.
☞ The branch will break free quite easily.
☞ Saw off the remaining stump so that it lies flush with the main trunk or branch. Trim off any leaves from cut branches and save them for the compost.

Keeping the lawn in tip-top condition

LAWN MAINTENANCE

55

Lawns don't just look after themselves; they need lots of tender loving care if you want them to stay green and pleasant. Mowing is probably the first thing that comes to mind, but don't mow every week come what may; you need only trim the grass when it needs it. A scalped lawn will quickly go brown in hot weather. As a general rule of thumb, remove about ¾ in. each time. I take the quick back-and-sides approach, but you could go for stripes or checkered patterns if you really have a lot of time on your hands.

If neighbors' animals have got into the habit of using your lovely lawn at their convenience, make sure that your fences and gates are secure and that there are no big gaps through which your unwelcome visitors can squeeze. If the problem persists, buy a chemical deterrent from a garden center. These products are not harmful, but they have odors that are unpleasant to the relevant animals.

TIP

Remember, earthworms are great! Their burrows run deep into the ground, creating good drainage channels and aerating the soil.

❶ Aerate the lawn from time to time using a garden fork. Put on your boots and place the tines of the fork on the surface of the ground.

❷ Press the fork down firmly with the sole of your foot and wiggle it back and forth a little to create holes in the soil—this will encourage drainage and air flow in the lawn. Do this at intervals of about 12 in. You can also buy aerating machines for this.

❸ Lawns look absolutely fabulous if the edges are well manicured. In order to achieve this level of splendor, use an edging tool. Its sharp, semicircular blade cuts through untidy edges beautifully, leaving a nice, neat shape. You can also use it to make lovely circles around trees or shrubs, or sweeping curves around larger areas.

WARNING

☛ When using any electrical appliance outdoors, is of the utmost importance that you take all the necessary precautions to ensure your own safety and that of others. If you do not have a professionally installed, waterproof, external electric outlet, use an extension cord from an indoor outlet. Always use a heavy-duty cord, suitable for outdoor use, in conjunction with a Ground Fault Circuit Interrupter (GFCI). GFCIs automatically "trip" and cut off the current if there is a power overload. Be very careful when running devices with extension cords (for example, lawn mowers). Always hook the cord over your shoulder and mow forward with the cord trailing behind you, out of harm's way. Never, ever mow while walking backward—you might accidentally cut the cord.

TIP

Do you like daisies? I do. Weeds are a matter of preference. Decide what you want and what you don't want, and act accordingly. Get a spot weed-killer spray to deal with scattered patches of weeds without damaging the grass.

LAYING SOD

Sod isn't that expensive when you consider that it gives you a new lawn almost instantaneously. Buy your sod from a reliable source, and get it fresh. Be very wary of sod that looks as if it's been lying around on a pallet for a while; it might be yellow or brown inside the roll and will be useless. Sod is sold by the square yard, so calculate the area that you want to cover and divide it by the unit area.

1 The first thing you need to do is remove the existing sod. Use a spade to cut under the grass to remove the top layer. Make sure that the soil is relatively free of debris, stones, weeds, and old sod. Rake over the entire area to make a flat surface in preparation for the new sod.

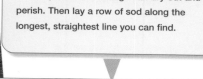

2 Begin by laying strips of sod around the outside edge of the intended lawn; narrow pieces at the edge can dry out and perish. Then lay a row of sod along the longest, straightest line you can find.

3 Lay the sod in a bricklaying pattern, so that the seams are staggered from one row to the next. Butt and push the ends together, but be careful not to stretch the sod. You can use a long wood strip to tamp the sod down after laying. Use an edging tool or a sharp knife to cut around obstacles or curves.

TIP
It is better to water thoroughly and infrequently, rather than giving your lawn a light sprinkle every few days. Water in the early morning and in calm weather to reduce evaporation.

AFTERCARE

Now that the sod is laid, you must water, water, water! New sod needs a good soaking and regular twice-daily watering in hot, dry weather. Don't mow the new lawn until it is well rooted to the subsoil, and then just give it a trim. Never cut off more than one-third of the grass's length. Resist the temptation to walk on your fabulous new lawn for at least a couple of weeks, allowing it to root down properly.

✳ DRINK UP BRAD, WE'VE GOT TO KEEP THIS SOD WELL WATERED!

✳ FINE, HONEY—AS LONG AS I DON'T HAVE TO SIT ON THE DAMP PATCH!

Making the most of your garbage

MAKING A COMPOSTER

56

Why not make your own compost? It's a great way to use vegetable waste such as peelings and trimmings; it's also ideal for grass clippings and fallen leaves. When you've finished your bush clearing and trimming (*see page 111*), you can save all the cut leaves for the composter instead of throwing them away (but don't include any branches). You can use your homemade compost for potting and general soil improvement in the garden.

need

* **lengths of 1-in. x 6-in. wood planks**
* **2-in. x 2-in. softwood strips**
* **1-in. x 2-in. softwood strips**
* **sheet of plywood**
* **screws**
* **tenon saw**
* **hammer**
* **jigsaw**
* **drill with twist bit and 1-in. spade bit**
* **screwdriver**

1 To construct the sides, cut two corner supports to size (*see Dimensions box opposite*) and then lay them parallel to each other about 32 in. apart. Lay six lengths of plank across them, edge to edge.

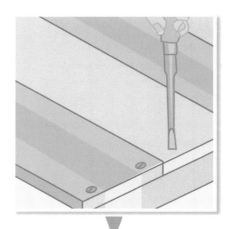

2 Screw each plank end to the supports. Make another side in the same way. Using the spade bit, drill a few holes at the center of the lower plank on each side. This will allow air to circulate freely.

3 Create the back by screwing six planks to the inside of the corner supports of each side piece. Use two screws at the ends of each plank to form a sturdy *U*-shaped framework. Turn the assembly on each side in turn to attach the tracks.

4 Screw a pair of track strips to the inside front edge of each side panel. Allow a space between each pair of track strips a little wider than the thickness of the planks. Screw the strips in place to form channels for the front hatch planks.

5 Slot the remaining six planks into the hatch tracks at the front of the composter. Don't attach them to each other; they can remain loose for easy removal when the compost needs turning or you want to take some out for use. To do this, remove a few of the top planks, then raise the lower ones enough to get your shovel in.

6 For the lid, construct a simple butt-jointed frame from 1-in. x 2-in. wood strips to fit the top of the compost bin. Screw the corners together and cut a piece of plywood to fit the top. Nail the plywood to the frame, and then cover the lid with roofing felt or plastic tarp to make it waterproof.

MAKING YOUR OWN COMPOST

Save vegetable matter from the kitchen and clippings, leaves, and soft vegetation waste from the garden. Pile it into the composter until you have a thick layer about 6 in. deep. Add a layer of compost activator, which you can buy from any garden center. This speeds up the decomposition of the vegetable matter. A thin layer of soil can also help at this stage; it keeps the decomposing matter warm and may add a few more good things, like worms. Keep layering like this to fill the bin. Turn the mass over after a month, then wait. In a few months you'll have lots of lovely compost at the bottom of the bin.

TIP
Don't include woody branches, tough roots, diseased plant material, or perennial weeds in the composting mixture.

Dimensions

Sides and back
Eighteen 36-in. lengths of 1-in. x 6-in. planks

Front hatch
Six 36-in. lengths of 1-in. x 6-in. planks

Corner supports
Two 36-in. lengths of 2-in. x 2-in. wood strips

Front hatch track
Four 36-in. lengths of 1-in. x 2-in. wood strips

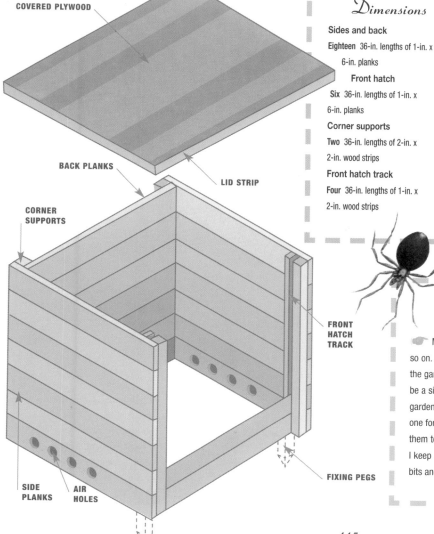

COVERED PLYWOOD
BACK PLANKS
LID STRIP
CORNER SUPPORTS
FRONT HATCH TRACK
SIDE PLANKS
AIR HOLES
FIXING PEGS

A RECYCLING STATION

Most household waste can be recycled: paper, glass, plastics, cans, and so on. You can do your bit to help the environment by setting aside an area in the garden for use as a recycling station. It doesn't have to be fancy—it can be a simple row of sturdy hooks along a sheltered and unobtrusive bit of garden wall. Simply hang up bags for each recyclable material: one for paper, one for cans, one for glass bottles, and so on. When the bags are full, take them to the nearest recycling facility. I have an old chest in my yard in which I keep a few small plastic storage boxes. I just lift up the lid and throw my bits and pieces into the appropriate box. Easy!

Getting down to earth
LEVELING GROUND

58

If you're considering a dry-laid (mortarless) paved or brick patio, or making a base for a small shed, this section is essential reading. The site must be absolutely level and well compacted before you begin—cheat at this stage and you'll be disappointed with the results. The advantage of dry-laid paving is that you don't have to build in a drainage slope. Rainwater will simply drain through the gaps between the pavers or bricks. If a fully mortared paved area is laid perfectly flat, water will gather in pools and you'll have a wet patio. Also, consider location: for sunbathing, your patio should face south or west, but if you're planning alfresco dinner parties, choose a shady spot (near the kitchen).

SITE PREPARATION

☞ Mark out the site using a mason's line and pins. Measure the area and place a pin at each corner (if your area is square or rectangular), and tie lengths of mason's line tightly between the pins. Check that the corners are at right angles. You don't need to set up formwork, or edging, for a dry-laid project as you would for a concrete surface, but it's a good idea. Nail long planks to wooden pegs and drive them into the ground along the perimeter of the site. The forms make a good containing frame for compacting and provide a straight edge when it's time to lay the slabs or pavers. You will then need to remove the topsoil to accommodate the depth of the pavers or bricks, and add gravel and sand layers so the top of the patio will be level with the surrounding ground.

1 Cut the wooden strips into lots of 10-in. lengths. Using a utility knife, whittle one end of each length to a point. These pins act as depth guides when you're applying the layers and tamping down.

2 From the top of each pin, mark the depth of the slab/brick, sand, and gravel layers. The sand and gravel layers should each be about 1–2 in. thick when fully compacted. To keep your clothing clean, kneel on a piece of landscape fabric. If the ground is very soggy, use a plastic trash bag because the landscape fabric will allow moisture through.

3 Use a hammer to drive the marker pin into the excavated earth. The top of each pin should be at ground level. Place a marker at regular intervals around the perimeter of the site, and at points across the area, too (if your patio is quite small then you can probably do without these).

4 Lay the long leveling/tamping plank across the top of the marker pins, and lay the level on top. Check that all the pins are level with each other around the edge and across the entire site. If any of the pins are standing too high, simply drive them into the earth a little further and check the level again. It is very important that these markers be accurate.

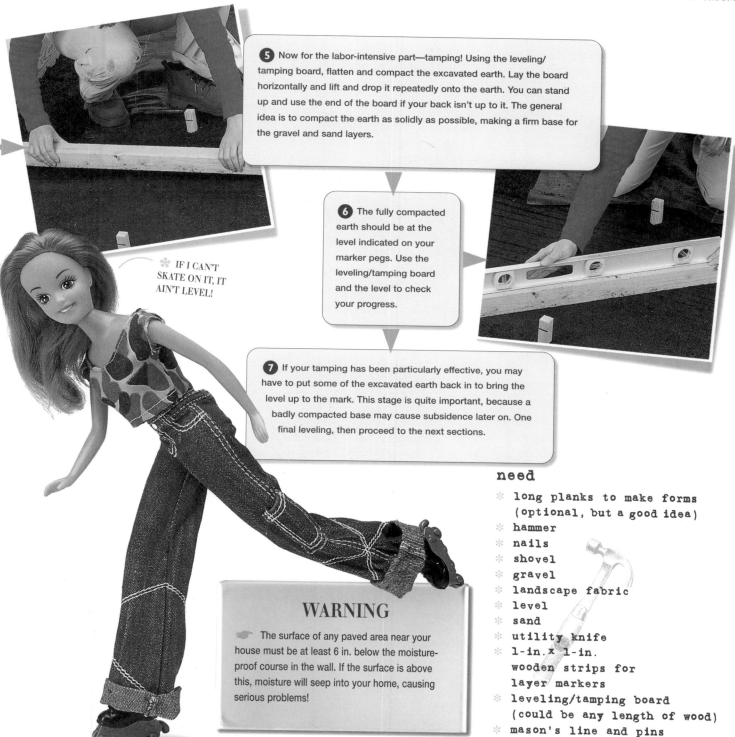

5 Now for the labor-intensive part—tamping! Using the leveling/tamping board, flatten and compact the excavated earth. Lay the board horizontally and lift and drop it repeatedly onto the earth. You can stand up and use the end of the board if your back isn't up to it. The general idea is to compact the earth as solidly as possible, making a firm base for the gravel and sand layers.

6 The fully compacted earth should be at the level indicated on your marker pegs. Use the leveling/tamping board and the level to check your progress.

7 If your tamping has been particularly effective, you may have to put some of the excavated earth back in to bring the level up to the mark. This stage is quite important, because a badly compacted base may cause subsidence later on. One final leveling, then proceed to the next sections.

✳ IF I CAN'T SKATE ON IT, IT AIN'T LEVEL!

WARNING

☞ The surface of any paved area near your house must be at least 6 in. below the moisture-proof course in the wall. If the surface is above this, moisture will seep into your home, causing serious problems!

need

* long planks to make forms (optional, but a good idea)
* hammer
* nails
* shovel
* gravel
* landscape fabric
* level
* sand
* utility knife
* 1-in. x 1-in. wooden strips for layer markers
* leveling/tamping board (could be any length of wood)
* mason's line and pins

Walk this way

LAYING A PAVED PATIO

59

Paving slabs are the simplest option for patios. The ones I've used here are the very basic man-made ones, readily available and inexpensive if you're on a tight budget. If you want natural materials, pretty colors, and/or elaborate shapes, then you're going to pay more. Spend a bit of time at a home-improvement store writing down prices, sizes, and types of slabs or paving stones, then work out how much it's going to cost before you start. Most stores sell decorative paving in kit form, so if you feel adventurous you could design something more stylish.

Estimating the quantities

Have a calculator at hand if your math isn't up to snuff! To calculate approximately how many slabs you will need, measure the length and width of your site, then divide each measurement by the measurement of the slab. Multiply the two results together to get the number of slabs needed. Alternatively, divide both the site measurements by thirty-six and multiply the results to get the area in square yards, then calculate the number of slabs using the quick guide below.

18-in. x 18-in. slabs: 4 per square yard

24-in. x 24-in. slabs: 2.25 per square yard

Buy a few spare slabs in case you need to cut some to fit.

1 Have your bags of gravel handy. Empty each one in turn over the compacted earth. Use the leveling board to spread the gravel out (you could use a rake if preferred).

2 Don't empty all the bags in one big pile in the middle if you're working over a large area; small piles dotted all over are better! When all the gravel is in place, begin to tamp down using the leveling board. This can be hard work, but it is worth doing well. Remember to check the levels as you go, using the level and the guide markers.

3 Cut a piece of landscape fabric to fit your area. You can use several overlapped pieces if necessary. Landscape fabric is an awesome invention; it allows water to pass through to the earth beneath, but does not allow weeds or other organic material to push upward, ruining your lovely patio.

4 Now for the sand layer. Follow the same procedure as for the gravel, emptying the bags in turn and raking or spreading out to cover the whole area to a uniform depth. Tamp the sand down firmly using the leveling board once again, checking with the guide markers as you go. Add more sand to any thin areas if necessary.

5 It's time to lay the first course of paving slabs! Begin by laying a slab in one corner, squaring one corner of the slab up against the corner of the form. Lay one complete row in this way using the form as a straightedge. You can also indicate straight lines with a mason's line and pins, then use the strings as your guide. If your patio is small, then you can space the slabs by eye, but use thin, wooden shims to create uniform spaces between the slabs if you have a large area to cover. Check each slab using the level as you go.

6 Continue to lay rows of whole slabs until the area is covered. If you have to work around awkward shapes, leave the slab-cutting until the end. Finally, check that all the slabs are level with each other using the leveling board and level, and make any adjustments with the rubber mallet. Make sure that you check the levels across the patio diagonally in both directions, too.

CUTTING PAVERS

👉 If it's possible to plan your patio so that you can avoid cutting paving slabs, do so—save yourself some time and effort! However, if your patio area does not allow this, you'll have to cut. You will need a brick chisel and a sledgehammer, a small wooden block, and safety goggles.

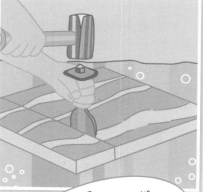

TIP

Most stores sell decorative paving—circles, semicircles, or shaped slabs, for example—in kit form. If you feel adventurous, you could design something a bit more stylish than a basic grid.

7 Finally, brush in dry sand to pack the gaps between the paving slabs, and wet thoroughly with a hose. This is the advantage of mortarless paving: any rainwater will drain away easily through the gaps, so you won't have puddles.

1 First of all, put on your safety goggles. Mark the cutting line across the paving slab with some chalk. Using the brick chisel and hammer, make a groove along the chalk line. Score the paving slab in this way on both sides and at the edges as well.

2 Place the paving slab on a bed of sand, and place the wooden block at one end of the groove. Use the sledgehammer to strike the wooden block while you move it along the groove. Eventually, the paving slab will break.

need

* **enough slabs to cover the area, plus a few spares**
* **gravel**
* **landscape fabric**
* **mason's sand**
* **shovel and rake**
* **brick chisel**
* **short-handled sledgehammer and rubber mallet**
* **brush**
* **mason's line and pins**
* **spacers (optional)**
* **leveling board**
* **level**

Make a bricktastic patio

LAYING A BRICK PATIO

61

Bricks make extremely attractive patio surfaces. They are much smaller than paving slabs, so there is greater scope for creativity when planning the area. They can be laid in numerous configurations or "bonds"—forty-five or ninety-degree herringbone, groups of two, interlocked end-to-end...whatever pattern catches your fancy (*see box below for some suggestions*). However, it is very important to remember that because bricks are smaller than slabs, they will need some kind of permanent edging at the perimeter to keep them from spreading out of shape. You can use decorative edgings or bricks laid end-to-end for this purpose.

1 Prepare the site for the gravel layer. Use a rake or the leveling board to spread out each load of gravel to cover the area completely. Tamp thoroughly using the leveling board, checking at intervals using the marker pins as a guide.

2 Make sure that all the material is well compacted and check it using a board and level. If there are any thin areas, add some more gravel and retamp. When you are satisfied, move on to the next step. Do not be tempted to rush the preparation stages, as it is important to create a perfectly level and solid base for your patio to sit on.

BRICK PATTERNS

Because bricks are smaller than paving slabs, the creative scope for layout is greater. Choose simple basket weave or herringbone styles like these or more elaborate styles. Remember, the more complicated the pattern, the more likely you are to have awkward-shaped gaps to fill when the design is complete!

STAGGERED BASKET WEAVE

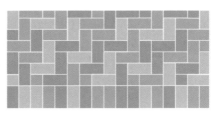

HERRINGBONE BOND

3 Cut a single piece of landscape fabric to fit the patio area if possible, or use smaller overlapping pieces.

Estimating the quantities

To calculate approximately how many bricks you'll need, measure the length and width of your site and the length and width of a brick. Divide one side of the area by the largest brick measurement, and the other side by the shortest brick measurement. Multiply the two results to get the number of bricks needed. Add a few more to the total to allow for cutting and breakages. Or, divide both site measurements by thirty-six and multiply the results to get the area in square yards, then calculate the number of bricks needed using this quick guide: 7¾-in. x 4-in. bricks = 42 bricks per square yard.

4 Now for the sand layer. Empty the bags in turn over the patio area, and use a rake or board to spread the sand evenly. Then tamp the sand to a uniform depth across the patio, using the marker pegs as a guide. Check the level using the level and board, and retamp if necessary to flatten out any bumps. Add spare sand to thin areas.

TIP

Each brick has a chamfered edge on one side so that you'll know which way is up, and they have molded spacers along each edge, so you don't have to worry about that either!

5 Use the diagrams provided as guides or design a pattern of your own. This is quite a speedy procedure: it won't take very long to lay the whole area. I used a basic ninety-degree herringbone pattern.

6 Place a row of bricks end-to-end around the patio perimeter, or use decorative edging stones. By now you should have decided which pattern you'd like to use, so begin by laying whole bricks in an orderly sequence.

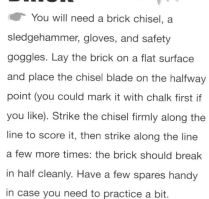

7 Finally, fill in all the remaining spaces with half-bricks or diagonally cut bricks (see "Cutting Brick" box below for a simple guide). When all the bricks are down, sweep dry sand over the entire surface, packing it into all the spaces. Wet the area thoroughly using a garden hose.

CUTTING BRICKS IS A GREAT STRESS RELIEVER —PRETEND IT'S YOUR EX!

need

* enough bricks to cover area, plus spares for cutting
* gravel
* landscape fabric
* mason's sand
* shovel
* rake
* brick chisel
* short-handled sledgehammer
* brush
* leveling board
* level
* rubber mallet

CUTTING BRICK

62

☞ You will need a brick chisel, a sledgehammer, gloves, and safety goggles. Lay the brick on a flat surface and place the chisel blade on the halfway point (you could mark it with chalk first if you like). Strike the chisel firmly along the line to score it, then strike along the line a few more times: the brick should break in half cleanly. Have a few spares handy in case you need to practice a bit.

Up the garden path

LAYING A BRICK PATH

63

Bricks are great for building pathways. Because the units are small, you can create different patterns—ideal for a simple straight path, and even more suitable for a curved one. All you have to do is ease the pattern as you progress along the path to fit the curved shape.

need

* bricks for path and edge, plus spares
* gravel
* landscape fabric
* mason's sand
* shovel
* rake
* brick chisel
* brush
* short-handled sledgehammer
* leveling board
* board to kneel on
* level
* rubber mallet
* dry sand
* small pebbles

* YOU MIX THE MORTAR AND I'LL MIX THE MARTINI!

1 Mark out a straight pathway with a mason's line and pins or long board, then excavate and compact the site between the markers.

2 Lay a row of bricks end-to-end along both sides of the path to contain the main pathway pavers, then lay the gravel, landscape fabric, and sand layers, compacting and leveling each layer as you progress. If the pathway is curved, use a hose laid out on the ground as a guide and drive in markers to follow the shape.

3 Using a board to kneel on, lay the bricks along the intended pathway in the bonding pattern of your choice. I used a forty-five-degree herringbone pattern. If there are bends or curves in the pathway, then simply ease the brick pattern around it.

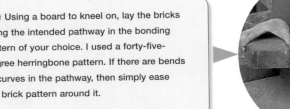

4 To complete the path, fill in the small gaps on each side. This may seem like a daunting task—it is in the nature of a herringbone pattern to leave lots of little triangular spaces. Do not panic, there's no need to cut triangular pieces of brick to fit: fill the gaps will small pebbles, gravel, or even colored glass chippings. Finally, sweep dry sand over the top to fill the gaps between the bricks, then wet thoroughly using a hose.

PUTTING DOWN A GRAVEL OR MULCH PATH

64

If your backyard is a little lumpy and bumpy and you really don't relish the thought of all that excavation and leveling, then what you need is a nice gravel or mulch pathway. Gravel and mulch are relatively inexpensive and look attractive as pathway materials. The soft top layer of the pathway will mask any imperfections on the ground perfectly, so there's no need to work hard with the level.

need

* bricks for edges
* gravel
* landscape fabric
* sand
* shovel
* surface gravel or mulch
* rake

1 Mark out the pathway with a mason's line and pins or long boards if it is straight. If you want a curved path, use a hose as a guide and drive pins in to follow the shape. Use an edging tool to cut along the marker edge to remove the sod if you need to.

2 Excavate and compact the site between the markers. Lay a row of bricks end-to-end along both sides of the path to contain the gravel, then lay the gravel, landscape fabric, and sand layers.

3 Empty the bags of gravel in the area between the brick edges. Spread out evenly over the pathway using a rake or leveling boards. The main advantage of using gravel is that it can cover a multitude of sins at ground level. Any small-sized aggregate, leaf mulch, or chipped bark would be a suitable alternative to gravel here.

4 When all the gravel is in place, tamp it down well using a board cut to the exact width of the path. Start at one end and work to the other, leveling out any really big lumps or bumps that you discover on the way. Keep a spare bag in the shed in case you need to replenish the pathway later.

AND

SITING A PATHWAY

Pathways with soft or hard surfaces get you from *A* to *B* in all weather without muddying your feet or wearing a nasty bald trail across the lawn you've worked so hard to maintain. If you have a new garden and need to decide on the best position for a pathway, wait a while and see where people walk most frequently, then put the path there. It's a waste of time and energy laying a path down one side of the garden only to find that it's easier to walk across the middle—people will always take the shortcut. Laying a walkway is simple—a sand and gravel base, along with a landscape fabric layer to prevent weed growth is all you need. Then choose your favorite topping for the path—bricks, gravel, mulch, whatever you like.

The path to happiness

MAINTAINING A GARDEN PATH

65

Maintaining the pathway you have created is a pretty important task, and not just for aesthetic reasons. Safety is also a major concern, especially if the pathway is used frequently. It is open to the elements all year round, and snow, rain, and the sun's heat all cause damage to sublayers and sand infills, giving rise to cracks and low spots. Also, in areas subject to freezing, dry-laid paths and patios are subject to frost heave. If your garden has an old pathway, regular maintenance is even more important; there is probably no weedproof layer underneath.

need

* old kitchen knife or putty knife
* crowbar
* mason's sand
* brush
* leveling board
* level
* power washer
* gloves
* scrubbing brush
* weedkiller spray

1 Get rid of weeds and unwanted organic growth between the bricks or slabs and along the edges. Pull out the roots ruthlessly—some weeds are seemingly indestructible. Show no mercy! Slide the blade of an old kitchen knife or a putty knife between the stones to hook out any stray pieces. Use the blade to scrape off moss, too.

2 Check that all the bricks or slabs are still level. Over time there may be a little subsidence in the sublayers, causing the surface to rise or sink. Sudden dips in the surface can cause unsuspecting pathway users to trip or fall. Lift uneven slabs or bricks using a crowbar and repack with sand, tamping down well, then reset the brick or slab. Use a board and level to check that the relaid slabs or bricks are level with their neighbors.

3 Now that the path is deweeded and level, use a stiff scrubbing brush to get rid of dirt, stains, fungus, or slippery organic material that may have accumulated on the surface. This is a problem that occurs mainly on bricks and paving slabs, and can be very dangerous if you happen to be walking along in wet weather. If you have a power washer, use it! It really is the best thing for getting rid of unwanted surface gunk because it just blasts through dirt!

TIP
If you are replacing old brick pavers, soak the new bricks in a bucket of muddy water to give them an aged appearance.

ANY EXCUSE TO PLAY WITH YOUR POWER WASHER!

4 If you have a persistent weed problem, then you may have to resort to chemicals in the form of weed-killer spray. The spray action means that you can direct the jet of chemical exactly where you want it, right at the weeds. These products can be used on lawns, too, because the jet can be directed to avoid the surrounding grass. To finish, sweep dry sand over the pathway to fill any gaps between the stones.

DEALING WITH TREE ROOTS

Despite their beauty throughout the seasons, trees can be the cause of big problems, such as subsidence or its opposite, heave. If you have mature trees growing too near your home, they could cause structural damage. The answer might be to remove the tree completely (*see box opposite*) or chop it back. Consider the positioning of new trees carefully. When buying saplings, ask how big they are likely to be when mature and the estimated root-spread area. Plant saplings about two-thirds of the distance of the expected mature height away from any major building or shed. Better safe than sorry!

Save chopped logs of tree trunks for firewood.

ROOT PROBLEMS

SUBSIDENCE Subsidence, eventually resulting in cracks in the structure of your home, is often caused by mature trees growing too close by. The roots can draw too much moisture from the soil, causing the earth near the house to subside. This causes damage to the house foundations, leading to serious cracks.

HEAVE This is the opposite of subsidence. When a tree is removed carelessly, the surrounding ground will absorb too much moisture, causing the earth to swell. This will cause displacement and damage to the foundations. Thus, it is very important not to chop down trees close to your home before getting advice from a professional.

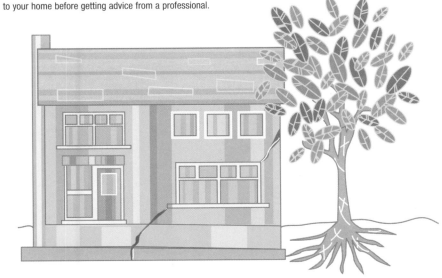

FELLING TREES

☞ If you have a small, unwanted, or dangerous tree in the garden, it is feasible to chop it down yourself. Don't just get the chainsaw out and hack the tree off at the base—this is very dangerous. You'll need a ladder, a big hacksaw, a lopper, an ax, a shovel, and a length of rope. Begin by getting rid of the small branches, using the lopper, to thin out the mass. Then, starting at the top of the tree, take the hacksaw and cut off the larger branches one by one. Now, from the top, cut through the main trunk in 40-in. sections, leaving at least 80 in. still standing. Now dig a 2-ft. trench around the base of the tree and cut through the roots, using the shovel blade if they're thin and an ax if they're not. Tie the rope around the top of the remaining tree trunk and heave. You should have sufficient leverage to uproot the tree and pull it to the ground. If the tree is big—that is, if you can't safely reach the highest branches by standing on a ladder—call in the professionals.

WARNING

☞ Some trees are protected. Check with the relevant authorities before felling.

☞ Warn neighbors before felling to keep them from wandering into the danger area.

☞ Do not sit or lean on a branch that you are cutting through!

Casting your own stepping-stones

67

CONCRETE IS marvelous stuff—I'm a real convert! It's cheap, readily available, and easy to mix, and the result is extremely durable and sturdy. However, it's also a bit heavy, so don't be too ambitious with size when you consider this project. The basic principle runs like this: make a mold, pour in the concrete mix, wait until it sets, and remove the mold...easy. I've chosen a simple heart shape but you can just as easily create a mold of your own, like a giant cookie cutter. The mold is reusable, so you can cast as many stepping-stones as you need.

TIP
Ask your local hardware store to cut a piece of aluminum to size.

need

* pencil and tracing paper
* marker pen
* sharp kitchen knife
* prepackaged dry-mix concrete
* old bucket
* piece of board to mix the cement and tamp the mold
* rubber mallet
* disposable latex gloves
* work gloves
* 18-in. square sheet of thick polystyrene
* strip of thin aluminum, about 4 in. x 47 in.
* duct tape
* releasing agent (light oil spray, such as WD-40; cooking oil will do)

1 Trace the heart-shaped template on page 183. Put on the work gloves and bend the aluminum strip to match the shape of the template. Tape the ends together with duct tape. Trace the outline of the shape onto the polystyrene sheet, then cut a groove along it with the kitchen knife to accommodate the edge of the metal shape.

2 Place the metal heart onto the polystyrene sheet and press the lower edge firmly into the cut groove. Wear the gloves for this—the metal edges can be sharp.

3 Take the board and place it across the top of the mold, then bang the board with the rubber mallet to make sure the mold is firmly embedded in the polystyrene. Spray the inside of the mold with oil; this acts as a releasing agent so that the concrete won't stick.

4 Place about one-third of the prepackaged concrete mix into an old bucket. Read the instructions on the package carefully. Pour in the correct amount of water as indicated in the instructions and mix thoroughly using the board.

✳ WHY ON EARTH DOES EVERYBODY CALL ME HARD-HEARTED HANNAH?

5 Pour the wet mixture into the mold; it should be wet enough to level itself. Now tap the sides of the mold to release any air bubbles in the mixture.

TIP

One fifty-five-pound bag of concrete mix will make about three stepping-stones of this size and about 1½ in. deep.

6 Put on the latex gloves and trace a swirl pattern (or a design of your choice) in the surface of the concrete using your index finger. Don't take too long because the mixture begins to set in about thirty minutes. Set the mold aside for a day or two.

TIP

Be sure to add the correct amount of water to the dry mix; the set mortar may be weakened if the mixture is overwatered.

7 You can now remove the metal heart mold; the concrete should be sufficiently hard not to need the mold. Remove the concrete stepping-stone and set aside for a few more days until completely set. The mold is now ready for reuse, so you can make as many stones as you like.

One small step...

SETTING STEPPING-STONES

Stepping-stones are less obtrusive than a solid pathway, and more decorative. Use them to lead to a cute bench in a sunny spot, or to a focal point, such as a pond or sundial. You could have pretty stepping-stones leading to the garden shed, simply for your own amusement! The other point to note is, of course, cost. A continuous solid pathway can be expensive; a few stepping-stones serve the same purpose for a fraction of the cost. In addition, a few well-placed stepping-stones can act as lawn savers; instead of laying a solid pathway, just set the stones along the track that gets walked on most often.

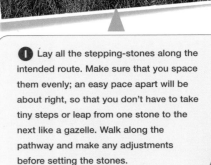

TIP
Functionality need not be the main purpose of a stepping-stone. You can buy or make decorative shapes that serve as focal points in themselves. You don't really have to step on them at all!

✳ WALK ON WET GRASS? IN THESE SHOES? WHAT ARE YOU THINKING?

1 Lay all the stepping-stones along the intended route. Make sure that you space them evenly; an easy pace apart will be about right, so that you don't have to take tiny steps or leap from one stone to the next like a gazelle. Walk along the pathway and make any adjustments before setting the stones.

2 When you're completely happy with the positioning of the stepping-stones, use the point of a trowel to cut through the sod around the edge of the first stone. Ensure that you make quite a deep cut so you will be able to remove the topsoil without too much trouble.

3 Now remove the stone and lay it near its intended position. If you're using natural or irregular stones, then it probably won't fit in another hole.

TIP

Ensure stepping-stones' surfaces are slightly lower than the surrounding ground so that your lawn mower will just skim over the top and path users won't trip.

need
* stepping-stones
* gloves
* trowel
* shovel
* mason's sand
* hand spade
* level
* tamping board
* mallet

Mason's sand

4 Remove the sod patch within the cut outline. The aim is to excavate the soil underneath to accommodate the depth of the stone plus a 1-in. bed of sand. The sand helps keep the stones level and firm. Ideally, the surface of the stone should be slightly lower than the surrounding ground. The reasons for this are twofold: to save your lawn mower and to help pathway users! If the stone juts out of the lawn, then the mower blades may be damaged and pedestrians may trip over the edge and fall.

5 Excavate each hole using a small hand spade, then fill with sand to a depth of about 1 in. Tamp across the surface with the end of the wooden board so that it is roughly level. The leveling process is helped if the sand is slightly dampened. If you find that your sand is too dry, simply spray with water using a plant spray after placing the board in the hole, then tamp down.

6 Lay the stones in the prepared holes, then walk along the path, checking each one to see whether it rocks or remains steady. When you reach a wobbly stepping-stone, place the board across its top and tap gently with the mallet to even out the sand packing underneath and stabilize the stone.

PEST CONTROL

Slugs and snails—they will eat everything in sight. Slug pellets are unpleasant but effective, but my favored method is the slug trap—yes, a good old-fashioned one. Bury a dish in the soil and fill it with beer. The slugs will be attracted to it, fall in, and drown—simple. There's always the option of the midnight vigil: stay up late, go outside with a flashlight, find all the slugs and snails that have come out to play, and pick them up (with gloves on!). Dispose of in a manner of your choosing.

* BROADS! YOU GIVE 'EM YOUR HEART AND THEY JUST WALK ALL OVER IT!

Making a bottle-bottom path

69

YOU'VE THROWN a party and your friends have kindly left you with lots of empty bottles. What can you do with them? Well, you can put them in a box and take them to the local recycling station, or you can get creative in the garden. Small glass bottles make perfect edgings for pathways or flower beds—all you have to do is soak them in water to remove the labels, then decide where you'd like the pathway or edge to go. Gravel paths are also a good solution if the ground is uneven. No need to use the level for this one!

* I GUESS I CAN DOWN A FEW MORE IF YOU REALLY NEED MORE BOTTLES.

1 Decide the location of your pathway, then mark roughly with wooden cleats if the pathway is straight or with pegs and string to indicate curves. Use the fork to loosen the soil a little in the section between the strings. Using a hand trowel, dig narrow trenches on either side of the pathway to accommodate the beer bottles, just inside the strings.

2 Place the bottles in a row, neck down in the trenches. Place the board across the base of each one and strike a few times with the rubber mallet to make sure the bottle is firmly embedded in the earth. The base of each bottle should protrude above ground level by about 2 in. on each side of the pathway.

TIP
You can use wine bottles for this, too, but you need to dig a deeper trench to fit them in.

need

* lots of empty glass
  beer bottles
* fork
* hand trowel
* bags of mason's sand
* bags of gravel
* tamping board
* rubber mallet
* rake
* spade

3 Take the tamping board and use it to tamp down the soil between the bottle edges. The earth does not need to be absolutely level, so you can march up and down the pathway in your rubber boots and let your feet do all the tamping if you like. The soil needs to be about 2½ in. below ground level to accommodate the sand layer and the gravel.

TIP
You can use landscape fabric under the sand layer if you like. This helps to prevent weed growth.

4 Carefully empty a few bags of mason's sand onto the tamped earth and use the board or a rake to spread the sand out evenly.

5 Now it's time for more tamping with that board, or marching up and down briskly if you prefer. For your path to look even, the sand layer needs to be of a reasonably uniform thickness: about 1¼ in. should be sufficient.

TIP
Bags of sand and gravel are quite weighty. Always approach heavy loads carefully, lifting from the knees so that you don't injure your back.

6 Finally, pour on the gravel layer. There are many types of gravel available in all sorts of colors and sizes—just take your pick. Use a garden rake to spread the gravel evenly over the path. Don't worry if the sand and gravel layers settle a little after a short period of time; you can simply level them up again with more gravel at a later date.

WHAT! YOU WANT ME TO DO ANOTHER ONE?

Welcome aboard

INSTALLING DECKING

Everybody wants a deck these days, whether it be a high-level deck to even out a garden gradient and create a new outdoor living platform or a low-level deck as an alternative to a patio. No special skills are needed and all the materials are relatively inexpensive and readily available at home centers.

PROJECT CONSIDERATIONS

What and where? Basically, decks fall into two categories: high level and low level. Use the basic low-level construction for flat areas, and high-level or part-raised decks for sloping gardens.

PREPARING THE SITE

Mark out the proposed deck area with a mason's line and pins. Remove any sod from the area and make sure that flat areas are leveled out completely. To keep any unwanted plant life from growing through the deck, lay landscape fabric over the site and cover with gravel if you choose.

BASIC FRAMEWORK AND JOIST POSITIONING

A deck basically consists of a wood frame around the perimeter spanned by supporting joists. Ideally, the joists should be no more that 16 in. apart. The framework must be supported from underneath by wooden soleplates, which in turn are supported by solid concrete footings sunk into the ground.

✻ SEE WHAT HAPPENS WHEN YOU SEND A MAN TO DO A WOMAN'S JOB!

SUPPORTING THE DECK

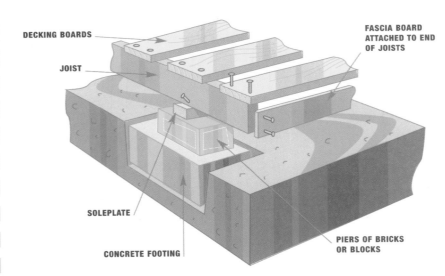

DECKING BOARDS

JOIST

FASCIA BOARD ATTACHED TO END OF JOISTS

SOLEPLATE

CONCRETE FOOTING

PIERS OF BRICKS OR BLOCKS

☞ You'll need concrete pads in each corner and at about 5-ft. intervals around the perimeter of the site, and perhaps in the middle, to ensure that no part of the deck framework comes into contact with the ground. Mark the position of each footing, then dig out a 12-in. square hole at each point. Fill the hole with a 6:1 aggregate-cement concrete mix, then allow it to set. Now build up platforms on each concrete footing, using a few bricks and more mortar. Use a long plank and a level to ensure that the platforms or "piers" are all level with each other. Now lay the wood soleplates across the piers and nail the deck joists to the soleplates where they cross.

WARNING

☞ This method of supporting a deck is for low-level decks in warm areas only. If the groundwater in your area freezes in the winter, concrete pier supports must extend below the frost line. Even for a basic deck in frost-free areas, check local building codes before you begin the project.

BASIC LOW-LEVEL DECKING

LOW LEVEL DOESN'T MEAN LOW QUALITY!

The basic support and framework construction is identical for high-level decking. The only difference is that the whole thing is raised on posts, securely anchored to concrete piers. The decking boards can span the joists at ninety degrees for a horizontal arrangement or you can go for a diagonal arrangement (but this means lots of cutting with the jigsaw).

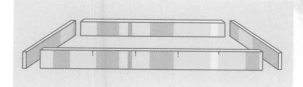

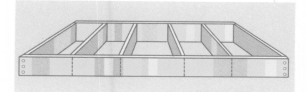

1 To create the basic deck framework, simply cut four joists to fit the perimeter of the proposed site, then nail together at the corners. Make sure that the corners are perfectly square, unless of course you are building a custom deck to fit an irregular shape. These four joists will form the front, back, and sides of the deck, and will provide a sturdy frame to which the floor joists and deck boards are secured.

DIAGONAL ARRANGEMENT

2 Now cut floor joists to span the framework, slot them between the front and back framework joists at intervals of no more than 16 in., then treat all cross-cut grains with wood preserver.

HORIZONTAL ARRANGEMENT

need

* drill and bits
* dust mask
* gloves and goggles
* saw and jigsaw
* spade
* hammer
* decking boards
* steel tape and level
* mason's line and pins
* cement and aggregate for footing
* 2-in. x 4-in. pressure-treated deck lumber for the deck soleplates
* 2-in. x 6-in. deck lumber for joists
* 6-in.-long exterior nails
* screwdriver and 2-in. screws

3 Screw the joists to the framework using predrilled and countersunk screw holes. Use three screws per joist end.

4 Cut the boards to size and apply wood preserver to the cut ends. Predrill and countersink all screw holes in the joists. Place the first board flush with the face of the front joist and screw in place. Position the next board, leaving a gap of about ⅛ in. Continue until the entire area is covered.

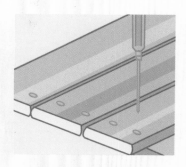

5 Use some decking boards as fascia panels to conceal the cut ends of the basic wood framework. Simply cut the boards to size, drill, and countersink the screw holes as before, then screw into position.

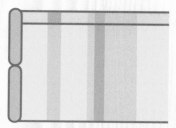

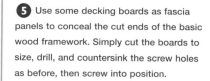

Keeping it all shipshape on deck

71

FINISHING AND WEATHERPROOFING DECKING

Weatherproofing your beautiful new deck is extremely important if you want the fruit of your hard labor to continue to look good in years to come. There are a great many clear sealing or staining/sealing products on the market now; choose a natural wood tone or a color to match your garden furniture. It is a better idea to choose a penetrating stain if you decide you want color, because paint tends to crack and peel eventually. Stains or sealants are easily applied using a large brush or roller with a long handle.

✳ WOOD STAIN IS NICE, BUT I'M PARTIAL TO PINK!

① Sweep the deck with a stiff brush to remove dust and dirt. It is advisable to scrub the deck with a mild solution of detergent to remove any previous finish. Allow the wood to dry before applying stain or sealants.

② When the decking boards are dry, apply an even coat of stain or sealant, using a large brush or roller. Pour the product into a paint bucket or roller tray.

③ It is important not to load the brush/roller too heavily since this may result in pools forming on the surface. Remember to treat any exposed end grains with the same stain or sealant product. If you do discover a pool or two, just spread out the excess with a clean brush. Do not allow the pool to dry or you'll get a patchy finish.

DON'T DO THIS IN YOUR FANCY SHOES!

need

* ✳ roller with long handle or large paintbrush
* ✳ paint bucket or roller tray
* ✳ stiff brush
* ✳ sealer or stain

DECK MAINTENANCE

72

Regular maintenance will keep your deck looking great. All it takes is a little time every now and then to remove debris and dirt buildup. Your deck will, if taken care of properly, last for years.

need

* rubber gloves
* bucket
* stiff brush
* small hand brush
* putty knife
* hose

1 Sweep the deck to remove any loose dirt and debris, then get to work with a putty knife. Slide the blade of the knife down between the decking boards to hook out any matter that may have lodged itself in there. Any blockages in the gaps between the boards may cause water to collect, eventually giving rise to rot.

2 Choose a good-quality deck cleaning product, put your gloves on, and get to work. Pour the cleaner into a large paint bucket, then apply it to the deck surface with a stiff household brush. Work the product into the boards, scrubbing away the dirt.

3 Hose down the entire deck now to wash away all the suds, taking all the dirt and grime with it. Begin cleaning close to the house, then work your way out toward the edge of the deck.

They call this fatigue duty in the navy!

TIP
When using the power washer, cover up any plants or shrubs nearby to prevent damage to foliage. Use a light plastic tarp for this.

4 If the deck has been neglected for some time, it may well be very dirty or have lots of algae buildup. Use your low-pressure washer to clean it thoroughly. Remember to wear your rubber boots or you'll get wet feet! Allow the surface to dry before reapplying any finish. It's best to do a job like this on a warm, sunny day.

How to make a big entrance

MAKING WOODEN STEPS UP AND DOWN TO DECKING

73

If you'd like to create an access stairway to a high-level deck or make steps to join different decking levels, then you can easily do so. Wooden deck stair stringers are readily available from most hardware stores and home centers. Stringers are the shaped side panels that are cut to follow the rise and run lines, and provide support for the treads (the horizontal part). All you have to do is attach the stringer to the deck, secure it to paving slabs or a concrete pad in the ground, then use deck boards for the treads.

❋ WHY DON'T YOU COME UP AND SEE ME SOMETIME?

COME ON UP! **INSTALLING STEPS**

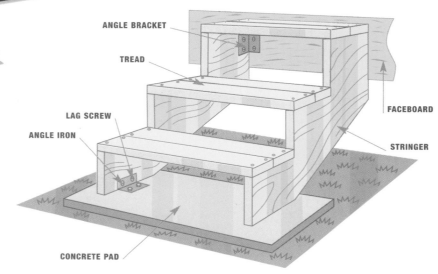

ANGLE BRACKET
TREAD
LAG SCREW
ANGLE IRON
CONCRETE PAD
FACEBOARD
STRINGER

❶ Decide on the position of the stairs and the area for the paving slabs or concrete pad. Either mark out the area on the ground with a mason's line and pins or just place the slabs on the ground and cut into the earth all around with a trowel. Excavate the sod and soil to a depth of about 3 in., then compact the earth with a board. Blend the concrete mix and water according to the package directions, then pour into the shallow hole. Level the surface with the board, then allow the mix to set. For the slabs, lay a 1-in. layer of sand in the hole. Then place the paving slabs on top.

❷ Decide on the width of the steps and cut the decking boards to that measurement to make the treads. Treat all end grains with wood preserver.

❸ Predrill and countersink screw holes in the ends of the treads, then screw each to the stringer.

❹ Now use the angle brackets to secure the top of the wooden stringer to the fascia board of the deck, and the base to the concrete pad/ paving slabs. Predrill the holes in the slabs or concrete pad with a masonry drill, insert anchors, then drive in the screws.

need

❋ two wooden stringers
❋ decking boards for treads
❋ drill with bits and countersink bit
❋ saw
❋ screwdriver
❋ screws
❋ anchors
❋ four angle brackets
❋ paving slabs or prepackaged dry-mix concrete
❋ shovel
❋ sand

REPAIRING CONCRETE STEPS

Over time, concrete steps may sustain damage due to wear and weather. This may result in cracking, flaking, or a general unevenness in the surface of the step, which in time can become dangerous and unsightly. Check steps periodically to make sure they are sound and safe. When the new cement is dry, paint the whole flight with a nonslip floor paint so the repair doesn't show.

need

* wood board
* saw
* few bricks
* sledgehammer
* bolster chisel
* trowel
* float
* goggles
* concrete bonding agent
* paintbrush
* prepackaged dry-mix concrete
* old bucket and pole
* thin sheet of metal
* short wooden cleat
* screw

* SAY DORIS, JAKE'S GOT HIS VERY OWN SLEDGEHAMMER!

* IS THAT ALL YOU WOMEN EVER THINK ABOUT?

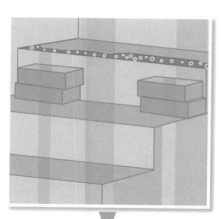

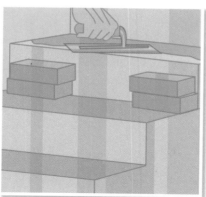

1 Put on your gloves and safety goggles. Using the bolster chisel and hammer, carefully chip away any loose material from the repair area to make the base stable. Cut the wooden board to fit the riser of the step to be repaired and prop it in place with a few bricks. Apply concrete bonding agent to the repair area using a paintbrush.

2 Following the manufacturer's instructions, blend a small amount of concrete mix and water in the bucket using the pole. Scoop up the mixture with a trowel and drop it into the repair area behind the board to fill. Use the float to smooth out the surface and sides so they are flush with the edges of the board and the rest of the step.

3 To round off the edge before the concrete sets, bend a piece of metal over the edge of a table to make an L shape. Screw the short cleat to the horizontal side as a makeshift handle. Slip the vertical side of the metal between the concrete and the wooden board. Slide it along the step to the other side. This will soften and round off the sharp edge.

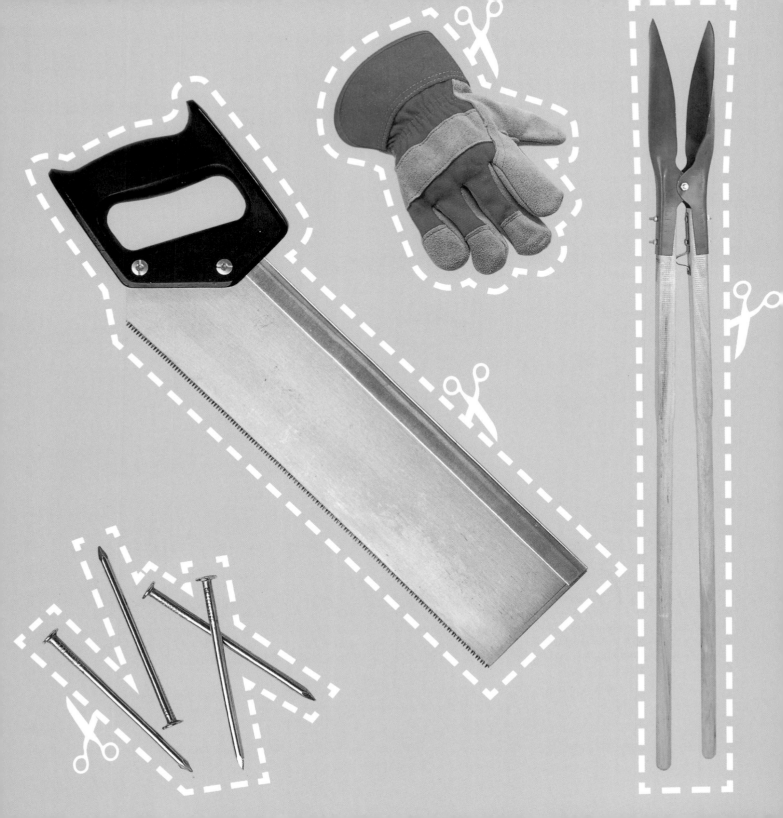

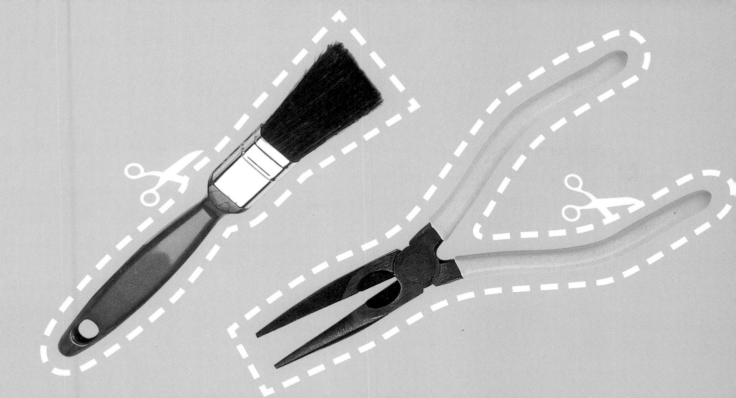

FENCING LESSONS

Whether you own acres of land or a tiny yard, you'll need to build and repair fences—read on to find out what to do and how.

Do fence me in

How to keep those wide open spaces in their place!

Decorative or functional, your fences should be well maintained, look lovely, and serve the purpose for which they are intended. One important thing to remember is—the neighbors! Check with neighbors on either side first before starting a fence project. You'll also need to check with neighbors if the new fence is to be higher or more substantial than the old one—it may block out light in their backyard. Finally, find out if there are any restrictions imposed by local building authorities—be a considerate fencer!

REPLACING A BOARD IN A FENCE

74

Closeboard fencing is probably the simplest type of fence. It is made by nailing vertical bevel siding boards to horizontal wood rails that are mortised into vertical fence posts. Each overlaps its neighbor and can be finished by adding a capping strip along the top edge. The result is an attractive solid fence panel. Softwood is the favored material for such fences because it is plentiful and cheap. Apply wood preserver or a stain to replacement boards—match the old boards as closely as possible or change the whole fence to fit in with the general garden decor.

need
* bevel boards
* tenon saw
* pencil
* wood preserver
* paintbrush
* galvanized nails
* claw hammer

1 Remove all loose or damaged boards and discard them. If the wood is rotten, then it isn't worth trying to save it. Hang onto ones that are not damaged. Now remove any old nails with the claw part of your hammer. Use one of the old boards to mark the length needed on the new boards, then saw each one to the correct size.

2 It is important that the freshly cut end grain of each new board be treated with wood preserver. You can stain the new boards to match the old fence after they have been secured. For a change of color, clean up the old boards, then apply your chosen stain or paint.

3 Bevel boards are tapered toward one long side, that is, they have one thick edge and one thin one. The general rule is that you work from left to right, keeping the thick edge on the left. The next board should overlap the thin edge of the previous one by about ½ in. Make sure that each board is spaced to match the old ones. Use a sturdy galvanized nail to secure it to the cross rail, making sure that it doesn't pierce the boards underneath.

CLEANING FENCES

Eventually everything gets dirty, especially outdoor stuff! Exposed to the elements all year round, fences can accumulate dirt, grime, and fungal growth, which, if left untreated, can lead to more serious damage, especially in the case of wood fences. There's just no alternative but to get the gloves on and start the clean-up operation. It's not a hard task, a little time-consuming maybe, but well worth the effort. If you've got a lot of wooden fencing, it's worth investing in a pressure washer, although they are fairly inexpensive to rent. Once you've used one of these wonderful machines, you'll never look back (and they're good for patios, walls, decks, and windows, too!).

need

* rubber gloves
* bucket
* bleach (optional)
* baking soda-based cleaner
* wire brush
* cloth
* pressure washer
* hose
* detergent
* rubber boots

A CLEAN FENCE MEANS A BRIGHTER YARD!

WOOD FENCE

1 Use a power washer to remove stubborn stains or unsightly fungal growth, especially on interwoven or overlapping fence panels. Put on your rubber boots before beginning because the water goes everywhere!

2 To achieve the best results, hold the nozzle of the pressure washer about 8 in. away from the surface to be cleaned. The power washer reaches parts that a scrubbing brush or cloth cannot—you can rent one fairly cheaply or save up and buy your own.

AND

1 If you don't have a power washer, you can clean a moderately dirty wooden fence with a household scrubbing brush. Fill a bucket with warm soapy water and scrub the wooden surface briskly—add a little bleach to the soapy water for very stubborn stains. Rinse the area with fresh water when you've finished. Do this on a warm, dry day so that the wood dries out properly, then you can paint or stain on the same day to complete the job.

VINYL FENCE

It's very important not to use a hard brush on vinyl surfaces. The bristles of a household or wire brush will scratch the plastic and cause permanent damage to the fence, so use a soft cloth instead. Before cleaning, it's a good idea to cover any surrounding plants with a plastic sheet to protect them. Use a solution of warm water and a household cleaner, which should remove all but the very stubborn dirt and stains. Do not be tempted to use any kind of bleach on vinyl fences because this may cause staining.

MORE CLEANING!!!

METAL FENCE

Cleaning a metal fence involves a tougher approach—a dirty or weatherworn metal fence needs the wire-brush treatment. First of all, protect any surrounding plants or foliage with a plastic sheet. Scrub the fence briskly all over with a solution of warm soapy water in order to remove dirt buildup and also to get rid of any flaking paint or rust patches. When it is dry, the metal can be treated with a rust remover and repainted so that it looks as good as new.

Your very own little house on the prairie

MAKING OR REPAIRING A PICKET FENCE

76

Picket fences are very cute and have a wonderfully traditional appeal—especially when painted white. I have some along the wall of my front garden just ready and waiting for the paintbrush. Lumberyards sell precut pickets in various lengths and designs, as well as premade fence panels. But, it's easy to make your own pickets for small repairs or for making a panel to fit small or oddly shaped areas.

need
* lengths of 1-in. x 4-in. lumber
* pencil
* ruler
* tenon saw
* sandpaper
* drill and countersink bit
* screwdriver and screws

1 Cut two cross rails to fit across the damaged area or between existing fence posts. Now cut the pickets to the size needed. At one end of each, use a pencil to mark the center, then mark a point approximately 2 in. down each side from the top. Connect the three dots with straight lines to form a triangle.

2 Saw carefully along the pencil lines, then sand all the rough-cut edges smooth. It is important that the points be smooth and free of splinters, not just for appearance's sake, but as a safety precaution in case someone should run their hand along the top of the fence.

TIP
To replace a picket, simply cut one the same size as the damaged one and screw in position. It is a good idea to make new screw holes in the cross rails and not use the old ones.

3 Mark the intended position of the cross rail on each of the pickets with a pencil. Make two screw holes set diagonally at the point where the cross rail meets each picket. At a butt joint, make two holes at each end of both pieces, making four in total. Countersink each screw hole now so that the screw head will lie flush with the surface of the wood.

4 Screw each picket securely to the cross rail (make a pilot hole in the cross rail first). Use screws instead of nails to avoid splitting the wood, but if you must, then blunt the point of the nail first by tapping it with a hammer. If there are to be joints in the cross rails, butt the ends together halfway across a vertical fence post or picket.

❋ MAMA SAYS YOU
SHOULDN'T PICKET
OR IT'LL NEVER
GET BETTER!

CHEAT!

ATTACHING PREMADE PICKET PANELS

👉 It is possible to buy premade picket fence panels. Measure the area carefully and make sure you purchase enough for your needs. It's better to have too many than too few—most hardware stores will exchange or refund cash for goods if they are returned unused, so keep your receipts. Cut the panels to fit in between existing fence posts or set new ones in concrete (*see page 147*). Hold up the picket panels to the fence posts and mark with pencil lines the position of the cross rails top and bottom. Screw two metal brackets to each post, then screw on the picket panels.

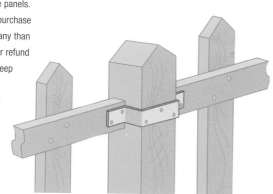

RANCH-STYLE FENCING

HOME,
HOME ON
THE
RANGE!

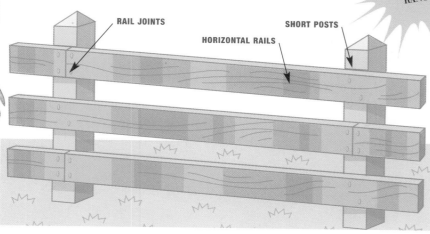

RAIL JOINTS

SHORT POSTS

HORIZONTAL RAILS

👉 Ranch-style post-and-nail fencing serves well as a low-level boundary where no privacy is required—or where there are no small children or pets to keep in! Simply screw horizontal cross rails to existing fence posts, or set new ones in concrete (*see page 147*). Butt the cross rails together halfway across a fence post. Also, make sure that the joints are staggered—don't place all the joints on one post. This way there won't be any weak spots in the fence construction.

TIP
If mending or replacing a portion of cross rail, then reinforce the joint with a metal fixing bracket.

Does your entrance let you down?

REHANGING A GATE

77

A broken or damaged gate is so annoying. Mine was hung with steel hinges that quickly became rusty and eventually seized up completely, causing the fence post on the hinge side to work loose. The only answer is to use brass hinges and screws. They're a little more expensive than steel ones, but they won't rust and you'll save yourself time and effort in the future.

1 Remove all the old rusty hinges and any other fittings, such as the gate latch, and discard them. If it is a particularly bad case of rust, then you may have to work really hard to get the screws out. If you're having trouble, try tapping the head of the screw first, then unscrew it—this can loosen it up a bit.

2 Locate the points through which the post is attached to the wall. Tighten the screws first to see if that holds the post more solidly to the wall. If this has no effect, you may have to remove the gate post and insert new wall anchors into the old holes, or possibly drill new holes in the wall and through the post and reattach it.

3 It is unlikely that the holes of the new hinge will correspond with the old screw holes, so fill all the old screw holes with a good-quality exterior wood filler, allow to set, then sand smooth.

4 Screw the new hinge to the gate first, then hold up the gate to the old post. Use the wooden shims or prop up the gate with boards so it is raised to the correct height. Drill pilot holes first, then screw the hinge securely to the post. Insert the top and bottom screws first to keep the gate in position while the remaining screws are inserted.

5 Finally, close the gate in order to attach the auto gate latch. Place the latch part on the post and mark the screw holes with an awl. Do the same with the bar part on the gate. Screw both parts securely in place.

need

* screwdriver
* brass hinges with screws
* exterior-quality wood filler
* new auto gate latch
* awl
* thin wood shims (or boards to hold gate level when rehingeing)

MAKING A GATE

If your garden gate is damaged beyond repair, then the best thing to do is discard it and make a nice new one. You'll find softwood gate kits like this in home centers. When you open up the kit, read the instructions carefully and familiarize yourself with the pieces before you begin. A clear diagram will identify each component and the instructions will indicate which screw or fixing to use at each stage.

need

* screwdriver
* saw
* hammer
* nail punch
* wood glue
* measuring tape
* pencil

1 Determine the width of the gate. Cut the bottom rail to this width and the top rail 5½ in. shorter. Position the bottom rail in the cutouts in the hinge and latch posts. Make sure that the rail ends are flush with the post edges.

2 Secure the rails with the screws provided. Position the end of the top rail that has drilled pilot holes between the hinge and latch post. Then screw through the pilot holes in the posts to secure the rail at each end.

3 Lay the assembly on the cross brace, then mark the pointed shape at each end using a pencil. Mark also the position of the cross brace on the top and bottom rail. The bottom end of the cross brace must always be on the intended hinge-post side. Cut carefully along the pencil lines. Apply wood glue to the marked areas on the top and bottom rails, then reposition the cross brace.

4 Place the vertical slats on the assembly and space out as needed. Mark the position of each slat with faint pencil lines on the top and bottom rail and the cross brace, then remove the slats. Apply wood glue to the marked areas, reposition each slat, and attach with nails. Use a nail punch to sink the nail heads below the surface. Wipe away excess glue and let dry.

CURING A SQUEAKY GATE

☞ Hinges have a tendency to get squeaky and creaky over time, especially if they are situated outdoors—annoying for you and your neighbors. The simple answer is to keep the hinges well lubricated. A drop of oil every now and then will ensure that the hinges are fully operational and, above all, nice and quiet!

ALL GIRLS APPRECIATE A SMOOTH OPERATOR!

Divide and rule

INSTALLING A PANEL FENCE

80

Premade panel fences are easy to put up, making them a popular choice as a quick and cheap fencing option. Normally available in a standard 6-ft. width in a variety of different heights, choose an overlapping or interwoven style. The panels are normally already treated, so are ready to stain if you desire. Panels like these provide a solid and durable screen, and are ideal for areas of the garden where a degree of privacy is required.

1 Mark the position of the fence using a mason's line and pins. Drive in a metal fence spike at one end of the marked line. Place a small piece of wood in the socket of the fencing spike to avoid damaging the spike when you drive it in. The wood piece should be taller than the depth of the socket but smaller than the fence post dimension—this is to keep it from becoming permanently engaged in the socket. Drive the spike into the ground using the sledgehammer, making sure it is set square to the marked fence line.

2 Cut each fence post to size, that is, the height of the fence panel plus the depth of the spike socket plus a little extra to protrude at the top. Remove the post piece from the spike socket, and insert the new fence post. Use a level to check that the post is vertical. Measure and mark the position of the next spike, the width of a fence panel from the first, then insert the spike in the same way.

3 Attach two fence panel clips to each fence post using galvanized nails, one at the top and the other at the bottom. If it is a tall panel then you could use one in the middle as well. Slot the fence panels into position, then screw the clips to the panel.

4 To finish each post, attach a shaped wooden post cap. Simply drive two galvanized nails through the cap into the top of the post. This is not absolutely necessary, but it's a nice finishing touch and gives a professional appearance.

need

* fence posts
* fence panels
* metal fence post spikes
* mason's line and pins
* sledgehammer
* hammer
* level
* saw
* post clips
* screws
* fence post caps
* galvanized nails

SETTING A POST IN CONCRETE

As an alternative to using metal fence spikes, you can set fence posts into concrete. You can also use this method to anchor a metal clothesline post firmly in the ground.

need

* fence post
* prepacked concrete mix
* posthole digger
* level
* watering can

1 Dig a hole about 12 in. in diameter. The depth should be about one-third of the finished height of the fence. Use a posthole digger. If you live in an area where groundwater freezes, set the posts below the frost line. Allow plenty of time to do this so you don't feel tempted to take shortcuts.

2 Ram a layer of gravel on the bottom of the hole and tamp down hard. This will provide a firm base and also allow ample drainage. Now drop the post into the hole and fill the surrounding gap with the concrete mix to about 2 in. below the soil level.

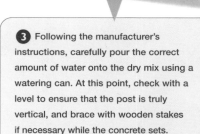

AND ERECTING A PANEL FENCE ON A SLOPE

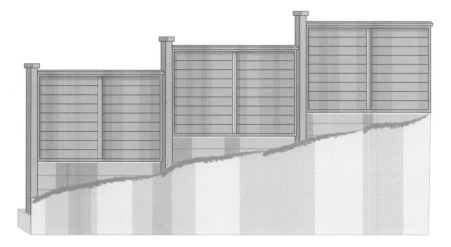

3 Following the manufacturer's instructions, carefully pour the correct amount of water onto the dry mix using a watering can. At this point, check with a level to ensure that the post is truly vertical, and brace with wooden stakes if necessary while the concrete sets.

 If your garden has even a slight downward slope, it will be necessary to set the panels in a series of little "steps" to accommodate the gradient. Mark out the position of the fence with a mason's line and pins in the usual way, then mark each fence spike position. Each fence post must be set vertically as before, but must be longer to allow for the slope in the ground. The shallow, triangular-shaped gaps that will appear between the bottom of the fence panel and the ground can be filled in with retaining walls.

Join the chain gang

ADJUSTING A METAL-POST CHAIN-LINK FENCE

82

Chain-link fences are typically built with metal end posts that have special straining wire winding brackets and right-angle intermediate posts at intervals in between. The straining wires that support the mesh are attached to the end posts by means of a winding bracket; each intermediate post has predrilled holes through which the wires pass on their way to the other end post. Over time, the wire mesh in these fences may become detached from the straining wires and lose its tautness and shape. Follow the steps opposite to get it back into shape again.

1 If the chain-link mesh has become detached from the straining wires, you can straighten out the mesh and then reattach it to the wire in one of two ways. Either use short lengths of galvanized wire twisted together, or you can just straighten out the top link of the mesh and then hook it around the wire. Use pliers to squeeze the hook shape together, holding the mesh securely.

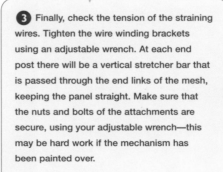

2 If the fence is more than around 3 ft. high, then the mesh will need to be attached to a third straining wire located at the midway point. This will keep the fence from losing its shape. Use twisted wire or small galvanized clips to secure.

3 Finally, check the tension of the straining wires. Tighten the wire winding brackets using an adjustable wrench. At each end post there will be a vertical stretcher bar that is passed through the end links of the mesh, keeping the panel straight. Make sure that the nuts and bolts of the attachments are secure, using your adjustable wrench—this may be hard work if the mechanism has been painted over.

* CALL ME OLD-FASHIONED, BUT SHOULDN'T THIS FENCE BE A BIT HIGHER?

REPAIRING A WOOD-POST, CHAIN-LINK FENCE

83

Chain-link fencing on wooden fence posts needs regular maintenance. The fencing is supported on two or more thick, straining wires attached to end posts by means of straining bolts. These bolts are passed through the post, then secured with a nut. The end of each wire is tied to the eye of a bolt. The wires are stapled to intermediate line posts and secured to bolts on the other end post. Adjust the nut of each bolt to tension the straining wires. If the basic wire mesh is sound but has come loose, you can easily straighten it out and replace the staples.

❋ THIS IS ANOTHER FINE MESH YOU'VE GOTTEN ME INTO!

1 Examine the whole length of fence and locate any loose parts. Secure the mesh to the horizontal straining wires at approximately 1-ft. intervals using short lengths of galvanized wire twisted together. Locate any loose or missing staples, then use long-nosed pliers to remove the loose ones.

2 If, over time, the fixing staples have worked loose, then the panel will certainly come away from the posts, and so will probably crumple and become distorted. Just put on your protective gloves and grasp the mesh firmly. You can now stretch and straighten out any kinks or folds.

TIP
While you're mending or replacing the chain-link fence, you could take the opportunity to repaint or restain the wooden fence posts. If a job's worth doing, then it's worth doing well.

3 Secure each end link of the mesh panel to the end post using new galvanized staples—don't reuse the old ones. It's also a good idea not to reuse the old nail holes either because the new staple will easily work loose and fall out.

need
* gloves
* fence staples
* hammer
* pliers
* galvanized wire

Protecting your territory

84

CHANGING A PORCH LIGHT TO A SECURITY LIGHT

An exterior wall or porch light is of more use to you and your visitors if it has a PIR (passive infrared) motion sensor built in that will automatically switch the light on when it detects someone approaching the door. The light switching on will let you know that someone is out there—friend or foe!

need

* PIR security light
* ladder
* wrench
* screwdriver
* drill
* wall anchors
* hammer
* wire stripper
* pliers

① Locate the old porch light. If you are using a ladder, make sure it is safe and on level ground before climbing up. Check the type of fastenings on the old light. Make sure you have the right tool with you before you get up the ladder.

② Unfasten the wall plate of the old light to expose the wires inside. You will see inside a plastic connecting block. Loosen the screws to release the wires—you can now remove the light fixture.

③ Unscrew and remove the old base plate. Attach the new base plate securely to the wall, using the screws and wall anchors provided— the wires from the main supply will pass through the base plate. Follow the instructions provided to connect the wiring correctly, then install the assembly securely in position. Switch on the power and test the light, adjusting the angle of the sensor to suit your needs.

WARNING

☞ Always make sure that the electricity is switched off at the main service panel before undertaking any electrical repairs or modifications. Do not dismantle electrical fixtures without turning off the power to that fixture's circuit at the service panel. If you need to use a power tool, then use a cordless one. Also, make sure you read the installation procedures provided with the appliance thoroughly before you begin.

☞ If you're not lucky enough to have an existing exterior light fixture, and would like one installed, ask an electrician to do it for you. This also applies to outdoor GFCI receptacles in sheds, or installing a weatherproof, outdoor GFCI receptacle.

SECURITY LIGHTS ARE ALSO USEFUL WHEN YOU ARE SEARCHING IN YOUR PURSE FOR THE DOOR KEYS, OR FOR GUESTS LOOKING FOR THE DOORBELL.

INSTALLING A SIMPLE WIRE-FREE ALARM

Lots of domestic alarm systems are totally wire-free and battery-operated! Most are purchased in kits with full instructions and test procedures provided. A basic kit includes an external siren, internal PIR motion sensors, and wire-free door/window contact magnets.

1. The siren is mounted on an exterior wall—use the backplate as a template to mark mounting holes, then drill, anchor, and secure to the wall with screws.

2. The door/window contact magnets are fitted on either the fixed or the opening sections—position the magnet at the extreme edge of the door/window frame.

3. Mark the outline of the mounting bracket on the mounting surface, then screw it into position. When the window or door is opened it breaks the contact, which activates the siren.

4. Install PIR motion sensors on interior walls at around door height so that the sensor is directed across the room. When the device is switched on, the sensors will detect the presence of an intruder inside and activate the siren.

MOTION SENSORS USE MINIATURE RADIO TRANSMITTERS TO DETECT MOVEMENT.

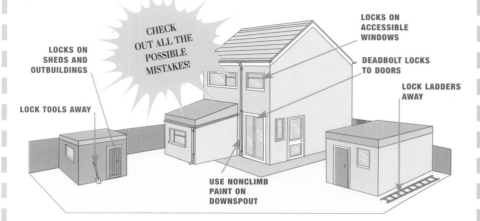

HOME SECURITY DANGER SPOTS

ON GUARD

CHECK OUT ALL THE POSSIBLE MISTAKES!

LOCKS ON SHEDS AND OUTBUILDINGS

LOCK TOOLS AWAY

LOCKS ON ACCESSIBLE WINDOWS

DEADBOLT LOCKS TO DOORS

LOCK LADDERS AWAY

USE NONCLIMB PAINT ON DOWNSPOUT

Installing an alarm system will add to a feeling of security in your home, especially if you live alone. In addition, there may be many areas around your home that could potentially provide easy access for an intruder.

Perimeter fences and gates

Make sure all fences are in good repair. If you have a gate or door, ensure that it is in good working order and is lockable from the inside.

Doors and windows Make sure that all doors and windows have adequate locking systems. There are many products on the market designed to meet any number of security requirements. Doors should be fitted with mortised deadbolt locks, in addition to cylinder rimlocks. A burglar will happily break a window to get inside, but after doing so will want to open the window to avoid the broken glass—don't make it easy, install window-frame locks!

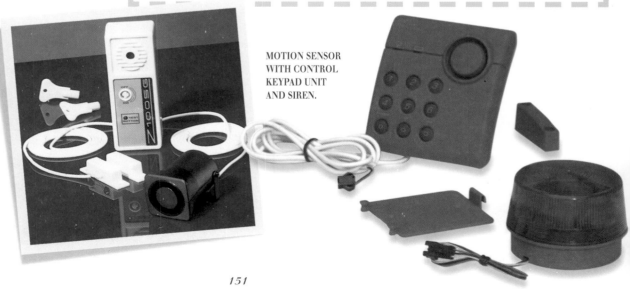

MOTION SENSOR WITH CONTROL KEYPAD UNIT AND SIREN.

Making an art deco–style trellis

86

ON A RECENT visit to a garden center I noticed how expensive simple trellis panels are! Rough-sawn wood slats are extremely cheap to buy, so I though I'd just go ahead and create my own. I took art deco architecture as my inspiration. Using a junk mirror as a focal point, I added a little shelf to hold some votive candles—these give off a beautiful reflection in the mirror when lit in the evening. You can secure your trellis in a suitable place for use as a climbing-plant support, a garden divider, or even a sunbathing screen. And try tying on a few fake flowers to the trellis just for fun!

❶ Cut the wood slats into the lengths indicated in the constructional diagram (*see page 184*). Clear a bit of space in your garden and lay out the vertical pieces, allowing approximately 6 in. between each one. Lay the horizontal pieces in position and you should see the trellis taking shape.

❷ Nail the slats together at each corner and cross point. Now place the decorative fan shape in position at the top of the trellis and nail securely in place. The trellis should be quite solid and firm now, so pick it up carefully and turn it over.

❸ Using the drill, make two holes on each side of the mirror frame, about 8 in. from the upper and lower edges. Drive a screw through each of the holes in turn to secure the mirror to the trellis frame. Now turn the trellis over again and lay flat as before.

GET YOUR MAN TO BUY THE FLOWERS!

4 Cut a piece of bevel siding board to fit across the bottom of the mirror between the vertical slats: this forms the candle shelf. Drill two small holes through the board close to the back edge and approximately 4 in. from each end. Drive a screw through each hole to secure the shelf to the trellis.

TIP

To use as a plant support, screw vertical wooden cleats to the wall first (drill holes in the wall, then anchor as usual), and screw the trellis to the cleats. This creates a gap between the wall and trellis, making it easier for climbing plants.

* MIRROR, MIRROR ON THE TRELLIS, WHO IS THE FAIREST, GO ON TELL US!

5 Lift the trellis into an upright position. You can attach it to a wall or use it as a garden divider mounted between fence posts (see "Installing a panel fence," page 146).

TIP

Never leave burning candles unattended, especially if you have decorated your trellis with fake flowers!

6 Place a few votive candles on the shelf. The flames will reflect beautifully in the mirror.

Basic pieces

Horizontals are numbered, verticals are lettered. See the diagram on page 184.

Horizontals
1: 19 in. (one)
2: 34 in. (one)
3: 49 in. (seven)
4: 16 in. (four)

Verticals
A: 59 in. (two)
B: 65 in. (two)
C: 71 in. (two)
D: 22 in. (three)

need

* ¾-in. x 1¼-in. rough-sawn wood slats
* piece of bevel siding board
* saw
* hammer
* 1½-in. nails
* drill
* brass screws
* junk mirror, approximately 16 in. x 24 in.
* votive candles

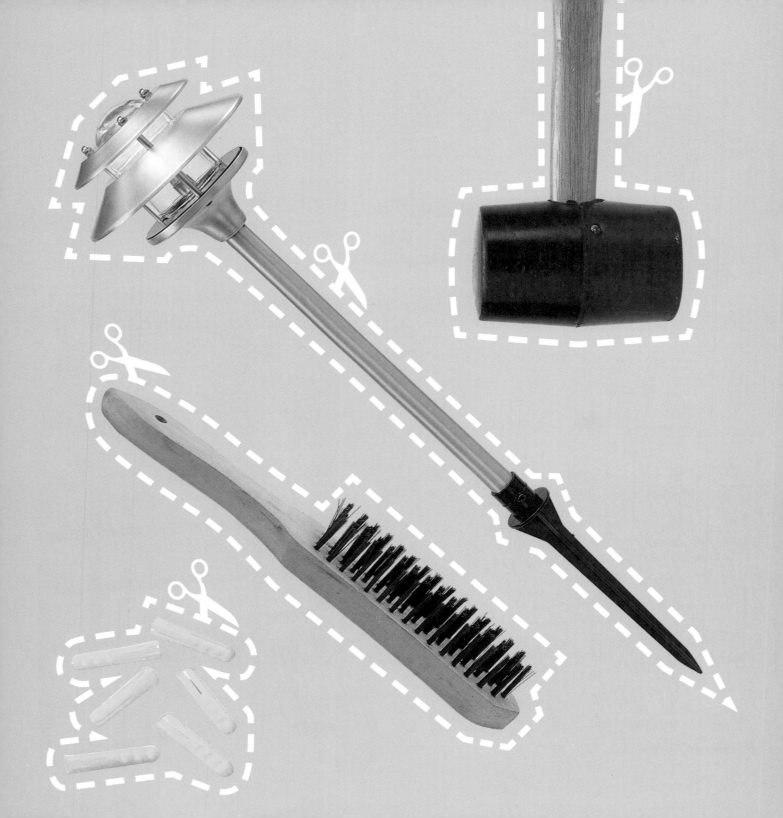

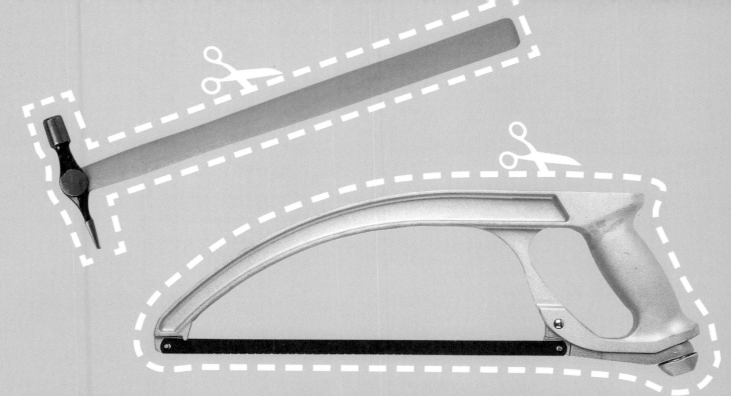

MAKING IT GREAT OUTDOORS

Now that all the repairing, digging, and fencing is done, get a little creative with garden fixtures, furniture, and features.

Finishing touches

Now that you've done all the serious yard work—digging, lopping, sawing, and so on, it's time to have creative fun in the backyard. This section covers all those finishing touches that make a real difference to the look of your backyard, including recovering a deck chair, hanging a hammock, painting and varnishing or weatherproofing wooden garden furniture, sprucing up plastic garden furniture, installing outdoor lighting and a water feature, cleaning and maintaining a barbecue, and making a wood bin.

REPAIRING A GARDEN UMBRELLA

87

Recovering a garden umbrella is easy. Remove the old cover and use the pieces as templates for a new cover. Use the leftover pieces of fabric to make pockets or ties. Remember to use a heavy-duty needle in your sewing machine!

need

* canvas fabric
* sewing machine
* scissors, pins, thread
* teak oil
* cloth

1 Remove the old cover from the umbrella frame and set aside. Clean any moving parts and wash the wood with soapy water. When dry, apply good teak or furniture oil to the surfaces with a soft cloth.

2 Cut out all the necessary shapes, including any pockets or ties, allowing about ½ in. for the seam. All you have to do is use the old cover as a template for the new one. You can make paper patterns for the shapes, or simply cut up the old cover into its component pieces and use them as templates.

3 (*See template diagram, page 184.*) Turn and stitch a narrow hem across the top and bottom edges of the four trapezoidal shapes. Pin and then machine stitch the main pieces together with the right side of the fabric facing upward. Fold and stitch the corner and center pockets into position. Turn and stitch a narrow hem around the top square flap, then secure this to the main part of the cover with fabric straps.

4 Unscrew the umbrella finial at the top and slip on the new cover. Pass the top flap over the finial screw, then replace the finial. With the umbrella closed, place the spoke ends into the corner and center pockets. When opened, the cover should fit tightly.

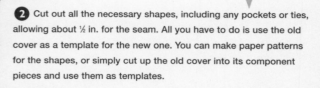

RECOVERING A DECK CHAIR

88

Have you got a few faded old deck chairs tucked away in the garden shed? Don't despair, and don't throw them away either—you can fix them up in no time! The deck chair canvas already comes in the right width, so you don't even have to do any sewing or neatening of raw edges. How easy is that?

❶ Use pliers to pry out all the old nails or tacks from the crossbars. Remove the old canvas and discard. At this point, it is a good idea to write a note on each crossbar, to remind yourself how to wrap the fabric!

❷ Use sandpaper to rub down the wooden framework. This removes any old paintwork or varnish and creates a good base for painting. When all the sanding is complete, wipe away dust particles using a cloth soaked in mineral spirits.

❸ If you're decorating bare wood, apply a primer before the final paint finish. Primer sticks to the surface of the wood and ensures good adhesion for the top coat. After priming, apply one or two coats of exterior-quality gloss enamel. Set the deck chair aside to dry. Some paints are self-priming, so you don't need to prime first with these.

❹ Lay the painted frame face-down on your work surface. Using the notes that you made in Step 1, wrap the end of the canvas strip around one crossbar twice, then use the staple gun to secure it. Pull the canvas taut, then wrap the free end around the other crossbar and staple to secure it to the cross rail.

✳ STRIPES ONLY BELONG ON A DECK CHAIR!

need
* pliers
* sandpaper
* mineral spirits
* cloth
* paintbrush
* primer
* exterior gloss enamel
* 50 ft. of deck chair canvas
* scissors
* staple gun

157

Making a hammock 89

OH YES! This is the life. Lazing in the garden after a hard day's work, shades on, cocktail in hand, magazine to read...lovely! To make this fabulous hammock, all you need is a length of heavy canvas (I chose a fantastic pink and red number), some eyelets, and a piece of rope. One end of the hammock has a flap with fabric ties attached; just roll up the hammock when it's not in use, wrap the flap around it, and tie it securely. It also helps if you have a nice, shady spot in your garden with a pair of trees from which to suspend the hammock! Getting in and out takes a bit of practice, but it's worth it in the end.

need

* about 10 ft. of brightly colored canvas
* sewing machine and thread
* eyelet kit
* hammer
* two wooden broom handles
* saw
* needle
* strong rope

ESSENTIAL TOOL! A DRINK CART.

1 Fold the fabric in half lengthwise and then stitch the selvedges together to make a tube, taking a ½-in. seam allowance. Press the seam flat, then refold the piece so that the seam runs down the center of the tube. Stitch across one short end, then turn the fabric through to the right side, just like a big sleeping bag. Press it flat, then mark the eight eyelet-hole positions (*see template diagram, page 183*).

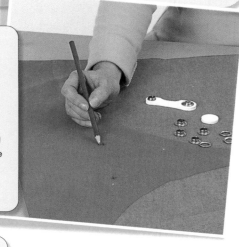

2 Following the instructions provided with the eyelet kit, insert eight metal eyelets at the positions marked. The kit contains a cutting tool and disk. Make a hole at each marked position using the cutting tool provided, then insert the upper and lower eyelet parts as instructed and hammer together to form the eyelet.

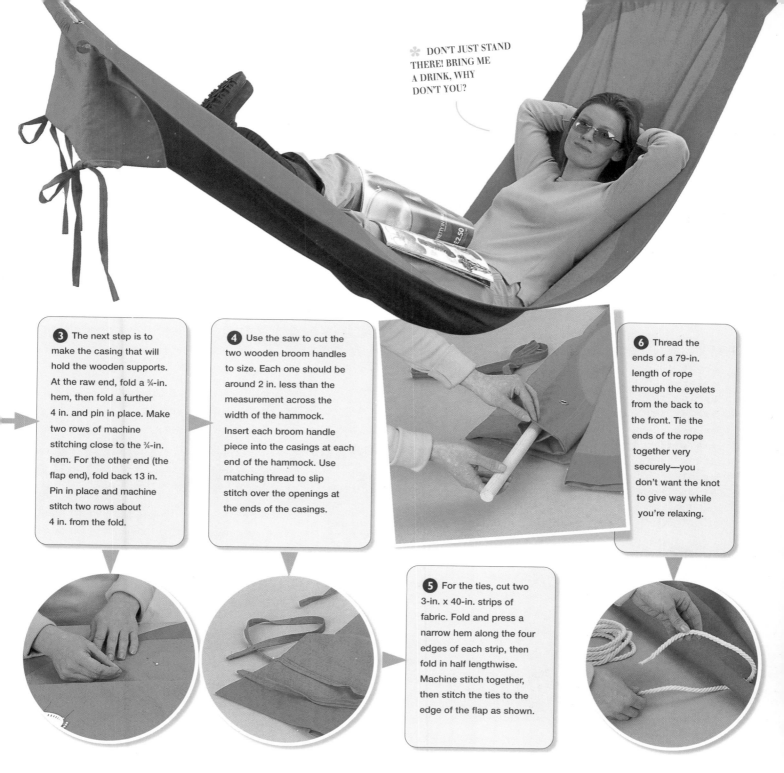

✳ DON'T JUST STAND THERE! BRING ME A DRINK, WHY DON'T YOU?

3 The next step is to make the casing that will hold the wooden supports. At the raw end, fold a ¾-in. hem, then fold a further 4 in. and pin in place. Make two rows of machine stitching close to the ¾-in. hem. For the other end (the flap end), fold back 13 in. Pin in place and machine stitch two rows about 4 in. from the fold.

4 Use the saw to cut the two wooden broom handles to size. Each one should be around 2 in. less than the measurement across the width of the hammock. Insert each broom handle piece into the casings at each end of the hammock. Use matching thread to slip stitch over the openings at the ends of the casings.

6 Thread the ends of a 79-in. length of rope through the eyelets from the back to the front. Tie the ends of the rope together very securely—you don't want the knot to give way while you're relaxing.

5 For the ties, cut two 3-in. x 40-in. strips of fabric. Fold and press a narrow hem along the four edges of each strip, then fold in half lengthwise. Machine stitch together, then stitch the ties to the edge of the flap as shown.

Sitting pretty in the backyard

WEATHERPROOFING WOODEN GARDEN FURNITURE

90

There are two types of wooden garden furniture, softwood and hardwood, and both will deteriorate if left outside for any length of time. Cosmetic remedies are quick and easy, and with a little regular maintenance, your garden furniture will serve you well for many years. Hardware may be prone to rust; remove and treat with a rust-removing product, then reinstall. It's a good idea to use brass or rustproof hardware and screws for outdoor furniture.

1 Hardwood furniture loses its beautiful dark color over time, becoming dull and gray. First scrub the framework thoroughly with soapy water and allow it to dry.

2 Now use a cloth or brush to apply a coat of furniture oil to all the surfaces. This will replace the natural oils and keep the wood from drying out. Allow it to dry, then apply another coat. Rub with a clean cloth to remove excess oil, then leave for twenty-four hours before use. Do this twice a year to keep your garden furniture looking fantastic! Softwood can be cleaned, rubbed down, then revarnished or stained in a wood tone or color.

* HEY, GIRLS! IF PLASTIC'S YOUR THING, THEN YOU'RE GONNA LOVE ME!

SPRUCING UP PLASTIC GARDEN FURNITURE

91

☞ Freshening up plastic furniture is easy. Use a specially formulated resin-furniture spray cleaner and a soft cloth to remove dirt and grease. Some cleaning products contain ultraviolet stabilizers to prevent colors from fading. Avoid stiff brushes or abrasive cleaners, because they may scratch the plastic surface. It's a good idea to invest in furniture covers to protect your garden furniture when not in use.

TIP
Don't attempt to repair split or broken plastic garden furniture. Recycle it (ask at your local recycling facility) and buy some new stuff!

LOOKING AFTER METAL GARDEN FURNITURE

92

Metal furniture has a nasty habit of becoming rusty when left outside and exposed to dampness and adverse weather conditions. Prevention is better than cure, of course, but if you find yourself with a few encrusted items, then it's a simple matter of derusting and repainting.

YUCK!
ALGAE GROWTH

Wrought-iron furniture weathers badly if left uncovered outdoors. Green algae can collect and grow in decorative nooks and crannies, not to mention the ever-present rust problem. The solution is easy. Scrub organic growth away with a stiff brush, use a chemical algae remover to inhibit regrowth, then follow the preparation, prime, and paint routine given here.

Wear goggles to keep rust flakes from getting in your eyes.

1 Use a stiff wire brush to remove all loose flakes of paint and rust from the surface of the metal. Treat any wrought-iron furniture prone to algae growth as directed above before painting.

2 Using a small paintbrush, apply an antirust product to remove rust buildup and create a smooth surface for painting. Work the product into heavily affected areas. Some products remove rust completely, taking you back to the bare metal. Follow the manufacturer's instructions carefully when using caustic products.

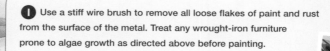

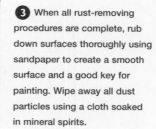

need

* wire brush
* rust-removing product
* paintbrush
* sandpaper
* antirust primer
* exterior paint suitable for metal
* mineral spirits
* cloth

3 When all rust-removing procedures are complete, rub down surfaces thoroughly using sandpaper to create a smooth surface and a good key for painting. Wipe away all dust particles using a cloth soaked in mineral spirits.

4 Apply a coat of antirust primer, allow it to dry, and apply one or two coats of an exterior-quality gloss enamel suitable for metal. Allow each coat to dry before applying the next.

Light up your garden world

FIXING UP ORNAMENTAL LIGHTING

95

Don't use indoor Christmas lights outside.

There's no point at all in creating a beautiful garden space if you can't use it after the sun goes down. Outdoor lighting can be both decorative and functional, creating a mood and adding to your sense of security and safety. Choose low-voltage systems, solar-powered lights, or the more traditional candlelit lanterns or garden torches—or a combination—to suit your needs. Solar-powered or electric lighting systems are convenient to use, but candles really add that romantic touch. A word of warning though, about nocturnal alfresco entertaining— beware of bugs! They love that flickering candlelight as much as you do. Be sure to have citronella candles or insect repellent devices operating so you and your guests don't get eaten alive. Also, hang a few strings of exterior tree lights around the garden for that twinkly enchanted grotto touch.

USE OUTDOOR LIGHTING TO ACCENT FEATURES IN THE GARDEN.

CANDLELIGHT IS SUBLIME ON A SUMMER EVENING BUT TAKE CARE, AN OPEN FLAME SHOULD NEVER BE LEFT UNATTENDED.

POSITIONING

☞ In general it's best to put outdoor lights where they'll be most effective or useful. If you have a pathway running through the garden, place little marker lights along the edges to shed a little light on your evening stroll. Outdoor dining areas always benefit from a few well-placed lights to enhance the mood—and to allow your dinner guests to see what they're eating! If you have a few fabulous plants, decorative garden structures, or a water feature, then a subtle light will create a cool focal point in the garden during the hours of darkness or twilight.

LOW-VOLTAGE OUTDOOR LIGHTING

GET THAT AUTHENTIC GLOW!

👉 Low-voltage garden lighting kits contain all you'll need to install a small lighting system in your garden. Some can be expanded with extra lights, cables, and connectors—refer to the manufacturer's guidelines for the maximum number of light units a single system will support. Extension devices are also available to increase the height of some globe and tier units. Because the voltage is low (12 volts), it means there is no need to dig deep trenches for the cables; a few inches of earth as a covering should be sufficient. All kits contain a transformer that steps household current down from the standard 120 volts to the required 12 volts.

Place the lights next to the intended sites, then run the cable between them, allowing a loop about 1 ft. long at each location for the connection.

Dig shallow trenches in which to bury the cables, then follow the manufacturer's instructions to connect each light to the cable. Now set the lights in place (most will have spikes to drive deep into the ground), bury the cable, then connect the system to a grounded outlet. (*See Warning Box below.*)

WARNING

👉 Always follow the manufacturer's instructions. Don't take any risks where electricity is concerned and never tamper with or dismantle any electrical fixtures or devices. It is advisable to connect the lighting system to the main service panel via an outdoor, weatherproof, GFCI outlet. The installation of such a device is definitely a job for a professional electrician. The rest you can easily do yourself.

Wall light

✳ JUST MAKE SURE THEY ALL SHINE ON YOUR BEST SIDE!

Tiered pedestal light

Globe pedestal light

Adjustable spotlight

163

Sizzle with style outdoors

BUILDING A BARBECUE

Build a brick barbecue in no time at all! This one is made from bricks stacked up in rows, one on top of the other—no messing around with mortar, either. The arrangement of bricks makes a really sturdy structure, but I would advise you not to build it much higher than the one shown. You can use any bricks you fancy, so long as they're all the same size. Light the coals and get cooking!

need

* Seventy-four bricks
* four paving slabs for the base
* brick chisel
* short-handled sledgehammer
* grill shelf from stove
* steel sheet approx. 18 in. square—ask a sheet-metal supplier to cut it for you

1 Put on your protective gloves. The paving slabs and bricks have rough edges and can cut or graze your skin quite badly if you're not careful. Lay the four paving slabs on a level surface to form the base for the barbecue. Take six bricks and lay them out in the pattern shown to form the first course. You can refer to the diagram given on page 185.

2 The second course is the same as the first, but rotated so that the bricks lie across the gaps in the first course. Lay the third as the first, and the fourth as the second. Alternate the rows in this way to build a tower of bricks ten courses high.

3 Now for the fire shelf. Take the steel sheet and lay it squarely on top of the tenth course. Lay another course of bricks, adding two half-bricks at the front. To cut a brick in half, place the blade of the brick chisel on the halfway point, then strike a few times with a short-handled sledgehammer. Then add another course like the first, but leave a gap at the front.

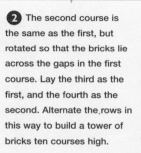

* WELL, I DON'T THINK IT'S CLEVER!

4 You can now install the grill shelf. Simply place it squarely on the brick tower, making sure that the corners overlap the bricks so that it's steady—you don't want your burgers to fall into the coals, do you? You can borrow a shelf from your kitchen stove for barbecue use, then replace it when you're done.

✳ YOU KNOW WHAT THEY SAY—IF YOU CAN'T STAND THE HEAT, GET OUT OF THE KITCHEN! USE THE BARBECUE INSTEAD.

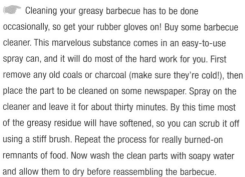

95 CLEAN IT UP

☞ Cleaning your greasy barbecue has to be done occasionally, so get your rubber gloves on! Buy some barbecue cleaner. This marvelous substance comes in an easy-to-use spray can, and it will do most of the hard work for you. First remove any old coals or charcoal (make sure they're cold!), then place the part to be cleaned on some newspaper. Spray on the cleaner and leave it for about thirty minutes. By this time most of the greasy residue will have softened, so you can scrub it off using a stiff brush. Repeat the process for really burned-on remnants of food. Now wash the clean parts with soapy water and allow them to dry before reassembling the barbecue.

5 Now add a windshield. Use the same format as the previous course—you can build it a little higher if you choose (especially if it's windy). This row also holds the grill shelf in place. Finally, place one complete brick in the space in front of the fire shelf to act as a primitive air vent. If you need more air for the fire, simply take it out.

Hang 'em high

HANGING A BASKET

96

Hanging baskets that overflow with beautiful, fragrant flowers are a joy to behold in the summer months. If you are an avid gardener, you can plant your own basket with your favorite blooms. If, like me, you are a lazy gardener (and what's wrong with that?), you can buy some lovely preplanted baskets from the local garden center or nursery. Now all you have to do is mount a secure wall bracket from which to suspend the basket.

need

* drill with masonry bit
* wall anchors
* hammer
* hanging bracket
* brass or antirust screws
* screwdriver

1 Hold up the hanging bracket in the desired position and mark each screw hole. Use the drill and a masonry bit to make a hole at each position. If you need to use a ladder to get access to the area, make sure that the legs are in a safe position so that you don't fall off!

2 Next, insert a wall anchor into each of the holes. The fit must be snug for the wall anchor to be effective, so you may need to gently tap them in using a hammer. It is very important to use the recommended bit size for the wall anchor.

3 If you buy a wall-mounted item in kit form, the manufacturer will usually provide suitable wall anchors and screws for installation. However, if the bracket is bought individually or you are remounting an old bracket, you will have to choose your own.

4 Make sure you have the screws in your pocket, then position the hanging bracket against the screw holes. Drive in one of the screws to hold the bracket loosely in place, then insert the other screws. When all the screws are in place, tighten each one. You can now hang up your basket of plants with confidence and pride!

* I LIKE MY MEN LIKE MY BASKETS— SECURE AND READY FOR DISPLAY!

166

MAKING A PERGOLA

Pergolas give shade to a patio or create a covered archway in a garden. To construct a simple flat-top pergola is relatively easy. The framework consists of four corner posts joined by two side rails, which are spanned by cross rails. The cross rails are joined to the side rails by means of cross half-lap joints. On this type of joint, pieces of the same thickness are notched to half their thickness so they can interlock and are flush when joined.

need

* drill
* hammer and sledgehammer
* tenon saw and jigsaw
* try square and pencil
* chisel
* screwdriver
* eight lag screws
* four 3-in.-square planed wood posts (tall enough to stand under!)
* four 3-in metal fence-post spikes
* planed 2-in. x 4-in. lumber for the two side rails and cross rails

1 Mark the position of the pergola out on the ground, making sure the corners are all square. Drive the post spikes into the ground at each corner of the marked area using a sledgehammer (*see directions on page 146*). Cut the side rails and cross rails to length, about 12 in. longer than the measurements between the corner posts. Use a jigsaw or wood saw to cut each end into a curved or sloping shape.

2 Lay the side rails on the ground just outside the corner posts, and lay the cross rails in position. Mark the position of each cross-half-lap joint along the top edge of each side rail. Mark the pilot hole positions.

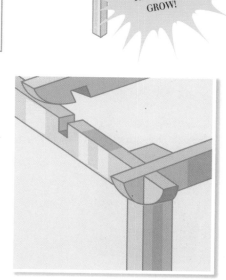

IT'LL LOOK GREAT WHEN THE PLANTS GROW!

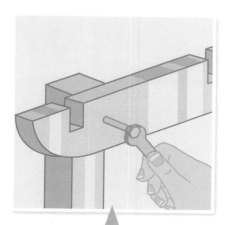

3 Mark out each cross-half-lap joint using a pencil and try square. Square down from each marker to the halfway point, then mark the across. Use a tenon saw to cut downward to the cross mark, then chop out the waste using a chisel and hammer.

4 Drill pilot holes in the correct position through the side rails and the first and last cross rails. Secure the side rails to the top of the corner posts using lag screws, then join the first and last cross-rails to the side rails and screw them in position.

5 Now take the remaining cross rails and simply slot them into position; the fit should be quite snug. You can screw them to the side rails from the top if you want more stability. Treat with wood preserver or stain to protect the wood from the weather.

How to keep your firewood dry

MAKING A WOOD BIN

98

If you enjoy sitting cozily on the couch in front of a roaring fire, you will know that having a plentiful supply of dry logs is a real advantage. This wood bin is easily constructed from pressure-treated rough-sawn lumber. It has closed-in sides and a tarp-covered lid and front flap. You can leave the lumber in its natural state or stain it.

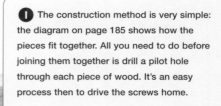

1 The construction method is very simple: the diagram on page 185 shows how the pieces fit together. All you need to do before joining them together is drill a pilot hole through each piece of wood. It's an easy process then to drive the screws home.

2 Screw four cross members to form the base of the wood bin. Try to space them out evenly, but you don't have to be too accurate about this. The pieces will keep the logs off the ground and allow air to circulate.

3 Cut lengths of bevel siding board to fit across the back and sides. Beginning at the bottom of each section, nail each piece to the wood framework. Overlap the boards slightly to form a reasonably weatherproof outer layer. Remember to apply wood preserver, using a small brush, to all the cut ends of wood.

4 For the lid, screw the remaining four pieces of wood together to form a rectangular frame—check at this point that the frame fits the top of the bin—then nail on the plywood panel. Lay the lid upside down on a large rectangle of tarp and wrap the edges around the frame, folding corners neatly as you go. Nail the tarp to the wood framework.

✳ ONE SPARK FROM ME, SISTER, AND THE WHOLE LOT GOES UP IN SMOKE!

5 Cut a rectangle of plastic tarp to fit the front opening, allowing about 4 in. extra at each short end. Cut a length of wood strip to fit the width of the rectangle. Wrap one short end around the strip and attach it with nails. The strip acts as a weight to keep the tarp flap from blowing around in the wind, keeping out the weather and keeping the logs dry.

6 Nail the free top edge of the tarp flap along the uppermost front cross member of the wood bin. Now place the covered lid in position. Your wood bin should now be pretty weatherproof, just lift up the flap to access the log inside the bin.

✳ KEEP YOUR LOGS COZY AND THEY'LL DO THE SAME FOR YOU!

need

* 2-in. x 2-in. pressure-treated rough-sawn lumber
* length of thinner wood strip
* drill
* 3-in. screws
* screwdriver
* saw
* sheet of plywood
* 1-in. nails
* bevel siding boards
* hammer
* sheet of plastic tarp
* wood preserver and brush

A Gaudi-esque mosaic garden stool   99

AS I'VE said before, concrete is an amazing substance (I really can't get enough of it!), and you can use it in small quantities to create decorative or functional garden structures. For this garden stool, I've used tubular metal frames from old stools as the basic skeleton, or armature, for these garden seats/plant stands. Simply pad the frame with polystyrene, wrap it in chicken wire, secure it with galvanized wire, and apply a couple of layers of concrete over the top. When the whole thing is dry you can apply a mosaic decoration in the pattern and color scheme of your choice.

❋ GIVE ME SOMETHING HOT AND SPANISH ANYTIME!

1 Remove the old seat from the junk stool. Using a sharp kitchen knife, cut two curved, roughly square shapes from the polystyrene sheet to form the seat. Wire it to the center of the tubular frame. Turn the frame upside down and press a polystyrene sphere onto the end of each leg. Turn right-side up.

2 Put on your gloves and use cutting pliers or tin snips to cut a large square of chicken wire. Wrap the wire over the seat and squeeze the corners down and around the legs. Use the thin galvanized wire to hold the mesh in place. Turn the frame upside down.

3 Cut four pieces of mesh about 16 in. x 10 in., and wrap these around the legs, covering the polystyrene spheres. Squeeze the wire mesh tightly around the chair legs and the spheres to follow the shape closely.

4 Pour a small quantity of concrete mix in an old bucket. Add water and mix, carefully following the instructions provided on the bag. Do not overwater the mixture because this will result in weak concrete.

5 Put on a pair of latex gloves and use your hands to spread a thin layer of the concrete mixture over the entire armature. It's a good idea to put the armature on a plastic sheet to catch any blobs. Set the concreted piece aside for a day or so to allow the concrete to set, then repeat the process, right-side up.

* IT'S NOT OFTEN YOU GET A CHANCE TO SIT ON YOUR ASSETS!

6 Use the tile nipper to cut the colored ceramic tiles into small irregular shapes, then use a knife to apply tile adhesive to the back of each shape. This process is known as "buttering—you can use an ordinary household knife to do this. Press the tile into position, following an ordered pattern or just randomly to make a free-form design. You could also add a few glass nuggets here and there to add interest.

7 When the adhesive is dry you will need to fill in all the gaps between the tiles. This is called "grouting." Apply the grout using a small spatula, pressing the grout into all the gaps and scraping off any excess at the same time. Wipe over the grouted surface with a wet cloth to finish. When the grouting is dry you can polish the tiles to remove any dust.

need

* tubular metal stool
* thick polystyrene sheet
* sharp kitchen knife
* thin galvanized wire
* chicken wire
* cutting pliers or tin snips
* four tennis-ball-sized polystyrene spheres
* prepackaged dry-mix concrete
* old bucket
* piece of board (to mix)
* work gloves
* latex gloves
* colored ceramic tiles
* tile nipper
* glass nuggets
* waterproof tile adhesive/grout
* cloth or sponge
* butter knife

Tinkle, tinkle, little spa

MAKING A SIMPLE WATER FEATURE

100

There's nothing more soothing to the ear than the gentle sound of bubbling water—a small, well-situated water feature makes a fabulous focal point in the garden. Get yourself to the garden center and choose a kit from the many varieties available. Most kits will include everything you need (except decorative details such as pebbles), plus instructions for installation. This one features a pump with a telescopic fountain so you can vary the height of the water jet. Now all you need to do is choose a site and dig a hole!

❋ WHAT? I'VE BEEN HERE FOR HOURS AND THERE'S NO FISH IN THERE?

1 The kit will include a container and a submersible water pump, plus fittings. Choose the site carefully. It needs to be pretty level to avoid too much excavation work.

2 Dig a hole that is large enough to accommodate the plastic container. You can also add a layer of damp sand in the bottom of the hole if you wish.

3 Drop the container into the hole. If it does not fit well, then take it out and dig out some more soil.

4 When you are satisfied with the fit, make a final check using a level—it's important that the rim of the container is perfectly level. Pack any gaps around the edge with soil.

5 Follow the instructions for fitting the water pump with the required telescopic fountain attachments, then place the unit inside the plastic container. Fill with water up to the recommended level, then close the flaps.

LANDSCAPING YOUR WATER FEATURE

☞ Once you have installed your wonderful water feature, create a natural look by landscaping the surrounding area afterward. Use some fresh sod cut to shape or make an arrangement of bricks or larger stones as a decorative edge. Pebbles and gravel are effective, but don't overdo it, because the arrangement should look attractive once the water has been turned off! A variety of small plants placed between the pebbles or miniature alpines planted in gravel will also create an attractive focal point. With a little luck the water feature will attract wildlife, too.

A WATER FEATURE CREATES A SPECIAL PLACE IN THE GARDEN.

EXCITE THE SENSES WITH THE SOUND OF TRICKLING WATER.

6 Wash all the pebbles in a bucket of water to remove dust and dirt. Once the feature is assembled, you can pile the pebbles on top of it, then turn on the pump and watch the water bubbling through. Rearrange the pebbles if necessary to make an even flow.

Decorate the surrounding area with sod or bricks.

need
* water feature kit
* shovel
* sand
* level
* pebbles

PUMP CABLE

☞ What to do with the pump cord? You'll need to run it unobtrusively from the feature to an electrical outlet. If you do not need to have the pump on all the time, then you can easily connect it to an indoor outlet. Simply plug in the feature to enjoy while sitting outdoors! If you would like the water feature to have constant running water, you'll have to bury the cables in shallow trenches running from the feature to a weatherproof external electricity outlet. This means that you can keep it running all the time, or have it linked to a timer. Remember: if you don't have an outdoor outlet, ask an electrician to install one for you! Dealing with main electricity is a job for the professionals.

OUTSIDE HELP

Now, what do you do when you do need a man and how do you know if you need one or not?

Calling in the big boys

We've had 100 things you don't need a man for in the yard. Now you need to recognize when an outside job is too big or dangerous for you and when it's time to call in the experts—we're talking major electrical jobs, roof repairs, and anything involving heavy machinery, girls. Before you start dealing with contractors make sure you understand the problem, know the jargon, and have a good idea of exactly what you want done. Then all you need to do is be a demon at negotiating a fair rate and a sensible schedule.

✳ WHO NEEDS A MAN...I'M QUITE HAPPY HANDLING LARGE EQUIPMENT!

TO DO OR NOT TO DO?

That's the question! If you're wondering about tackling an exterior maintenance project, then the first thing to consider is scale. Exterior home improvement tasks are slightly different from the interior jobs because there are more extremes involved. For example, a roof can be very HIGH, pavers can be very HEAVY, and outdoor wiring can be very DANGEROUS. If you have a knee-trembling fear of heights, then roof repairs are out of the question. Don't try to lay a patio using huge paving slabs. Compromise, use smaller, easily manageable paving stones that won't break your back.

My approach is more often than not budget-driven; you don't want to spend a fortune contracting someone to do a job you could easily do yourself. But, on the other hand, why kill yourself for the sake of a small fee? For example, you've bought slabs and sand for the patio, but do you want to do three or four trips to and from the home center in your car? Why not pay for delivery—for a few dollars you can save yourself a lot of time and effort. While we're talking deliveries, "to your door" may be exactly that—the door. If the intended patio area is at the bottom of the garden it's always worth asking the delivery person to take the goods to the site—smile nicely and tip well!

For the purposes of "not doing it," I've split large, pay-the-guy-to-do tasks into three categories: the High, the Low, and the Dangerous. Look at the lists when you feel a big project coming on or have an important repair to do, then examine your bank balance, grit your teeth, and get on the phone!

THE HIGH

In this category I have placed any jobs that involve getting up a ladder. Extensive roof repairs or replacements are definitely jobs for the big boys—they know what they're doing and will have all the right access equipment and skills to match. Window washers also have skills involving access equipment and chamois leathers. Don't risk life and limb cleaning upstairs windows if they're a bit high—just pay the guy. Also, window replacements and repaning large windows are definitely a home improvement don't. Last but not least—trees. Felling large trees is not a job for the untrained. Also, mature trees can affect the foundations on which your house is built. Never fell a tree close to your building without the advice of a tree surgeon, or, better still, get them to do it for you.

THE LOW

As for the low down and dirty ground-level (and below) tasks, this includes all work involving major drainage systems or serious blockages in sewer pipes, moisture-proofing, or repairs to moisture-proof courses. The foundations that your house sits on are pretty important; if you think you have a problem in that department, ask a professional for advice. If you're considering resurfacing a driveway or replacing a concrete basement floor, then get the guys with the big concrete mixers to do it for you. Small amounts of this stuff are manageable, but there's no joy in having to tote and mix huge quantities of it. Any substantial bricks-and-mortar activity like constructing an extension, a garage, or a shed for storage requires the skill of a trained craftsman. While a small patio is an achievable goal, a huge paved area may prove too much to handle. The same is true of major excavation work. If you have a big sloping garden to level, hire a man with the right machinery to move the earth for you!

SO GET ONE IF...

☞ extensive roof repairs or replacements are needed.

☞ large windows need replacing and repaning.

☞ mature trees need felling.

☞ there are major blockages in drainage systems or sewer pipes.

☞ a moisture-proof course is needed.

☞ resurfacing an entire floor or driveway is needed.

☞ major modifications or repair to the water supply are needed.

☞ a large expanse of land needs leveling.

☞ major electrical wiring jobs need doing—especially those involving water at the same time, such as the timer for the sprinkler system or a waterproof outdoor electrical outlet.

❋ LET ME DO THE HEAVY DANGEROUS STUFF!

HE'S YOUR KNIGHT IN SHINING ARMOR!

THE DANGEROUS

This covers anything to do with the main power or water supply. Dig trenches yourself, but any connections, modifications, or repairs to any major service supply should be carried out by a qualified person. All major wiring jobs, such as running permanent power cables to sheds, sophisticated security devices and systems, or automatic garage door openers, should always be installed by recommended technicians. These are expensive and really need to be dealt with by an expert.

177

HOW TO GET A MAN IN

Finding the right man may be a problem if you don't know how and where to look. A reliable, skilled contractor is a real find. Ask anyone who's ever engaged the services of a professional. Your first avenue of investigation should be your friends—a personal recommendation is better than any reference written on paper. Just put the word out that you're looking, then wait to see what happens. The phone book can be a good source of information. Jot down some names, then make some inquiries. However, before you speak to anyone directly, be sure to make a list of crucial questions to ask. Can he do the job? When can he

do the job? How much will he charge for the job? Can he give you a written estimate? Will he guarantee the work? Also, make sure you know exactly what you need doing. Be specific—it'll save time in the long run. Do a bit of research, familiarize yourself with the terminology, and learn correct names for things so you won't be umm-ing and ahh-ing on the phone. It's a clear signal to an unscrupulous contractor that you don't know what you're talking about and you can be completely taken for a ride. Don't fall into that trap!

So you've compiled a short list, what next? Well, the cheapest may not be the best. Then again, the most expensive may not be the best, either—so the one offering a midpriced estimate is probably a good choice.

* HE'S GORGEOUS, BUT I WON'T LET HIM KNOW UNTIL THE JOB'S FINISHED!

CHECK OUT THE GOODS THOROUGHLY BEFORE PAYING, LADIES!

Finally, check any accreditations. If your chosen guy says he belongs to a certain association or has any fancy letters after his name, it's a good idea that you make sure that they're for real before you shake hands and clinch the deal!

AND WHEN HE'S IN

Well done, you've hired your man! It's a good idea to confirm this in writing just as a safeguard. If it's a fairly substantial job, then ask him to draw up a contract stating the job description and any terms of agreement. That way both parties know exactly where they stand and have a piece of paper to wave if things go wrong (and he can do the waving too if you don't keep your half of the deal!). The contract should include a payment schedule, which you both agree to before work starts. You may be required to put some money up front to pay for materials and so on, or split the agreed fee into portions, payable when a certain amount of work has been completed to your satisfaction.

At this point, double-check that you're both speaking the same language. That is, try to supply him with all the information that he may need: words and pictures, plans, color swatches, and material samples, to make sure there are no mistakes or misunderstandings. After all, he's being paid to do a job, not to be a mind reader, and if he's badly or ambiguously briefed, then it really isn't his fault. If there's any change to the original plan, however small, then make sure he knows that he should consult you first.

KEEPING IT RUNNING SMOOTHLY

When any decorating, maintenance, or installation procedure is underway, then you can be sure that a certain amount of dirt will follow. Don't despair, this is normal, even if you do it yourself, but you can make life easy for yourself (and your workman). If, for example, there is no side access to the backyard, cover areas indoors with plastic tarps or drop cloths—you don't want a muddy trail through your house, and the poor guy doesn't want to have to worry about tiptoeing down your hallway either. Also, make sure that he's familiar with everything he may need access to and that he has your contact number if a problem arises and you need to be consulted. Also, be flexible. There are many things that are beyond anyone's control, so don't lose your cool if a mishap or delay occurs that really isn't anyone's fault. So long as you maintain good communication channels with your workman, there shouldn't be any problems.

Another important point to mention before you begin major, messy, or noisy jobs, either by yourself or using a contractor, is to speak to your neighbors. Let them know what you intend to do and when, then agree to acceptable "noise-making" hours. It pays to stay on good terms with the folks next door.

OK. He has his instructions, he knows what he's doing, you're happy, he's happy—now make sure that you have plenty of coffee and cookies to keep him going and leave him alone to get down to it!

ANATOMY LESSONS
GETTING DOWN TO IT

A wonderful specimen—ready, willing, and able! Congratulate yourself on choosing the best man for the job. Keep him well wired with coffee and cookies, and you'll not be disappointed. If he proves to be really good then get a bunch of his business cards and distribute them among neighbors and friends —contractors rely on their good reputation.

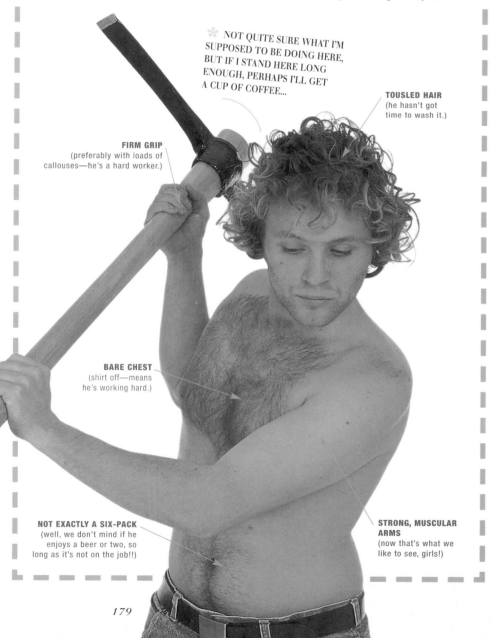

*NOT QUITE SURE WHAT I'M SUPPOSED TO BE DOING HERE, BUT IF I STAND HERE LONG ENOUGH, PERHAPS I'LL GET A CUP OF COFFEE...

TOUSLED HAIR (he hasn't got time to wash it.)

FIRM GRIP (preferably with loads of callouses—he's a hard worker.)

BARE CHEST (shirt off—means he's working hard.)

STRONG, MUSCULAR ARMS (now that's what we like to see, girls!)

NOT EXACTLY A SIX-PACK (well, we don't mind if he enjoys a beer or two, so long as it's not on the job!!)

179

Yard and exterior checklist

USE THIS checklist as a handy reminder of what to do, where to do it, and when to do it—and also to keep track of when you did it last. Make sure you don't do more work than necessary, girls! Keep all your notes in a safe place so that you can easily refer to them when the time comes for regular maintenance procedures, or an emergency arises.

WHAT AND WHEN?

Make dated notes of monthly and annual checks and routine maintenance—prevention is always better than cure.

DRAINS	ROOF AND GUTTERS	WINDOWS AND DOORS	SECURITY SYSTEMS	EXTERIOR DECORATION
			Change batteries if cordless	

WATER FEATURE PUMP/ SPRINKLER SYSTEM	GARAGE DOOR OPENING MECHANISM	BULB PLANTING	GATES AND FENCES	COMPOST
		What and where		When started, when to turn

WHO

Keep a record of work, repairs, or replacements done—and keep any receipts or guarantees. Most guarantees are transferable to a new owner if you sell your house. You need names, phone numbers, and dates, for example.

KEEP SAFE

Keep important documents such as operation manuals, receipts, and guarantees for equipment or works carried out. Garden plans, sprinkler system routes, notes on quantities and materials, paint color codes, and suppliers, etc. could all be useful at a later date when the time comes for a simple repair.

MOISTURE-PROOF COURSE	ROOF REPAIRS/REPLACEMENTS	WINDOW REPLACEMENTS/REPAIRS	SECURITY/SPRINKLER SYSTEM INSTALLATION	BUILDING WORK

DRAINAGE	BUILDING WORK	GARDEN EQUIPMENT SERVICE/REPAIR	OUTDOOR ELECTRICAL OUTLETS	TREE REMOVAL/TREATMENT

A girl can always use a little guidance

TEMPLATES

Here are scaled-down templates, patterns, and constructional diagrams to help you complete all the creative projects in this book.

☛ Cut out two fronts and two backs, then construct the birdhouse using wood glue, nails, and cleats cut to size as shown.

FRONT

SIDE

Making a birdhouse, pages 106–107

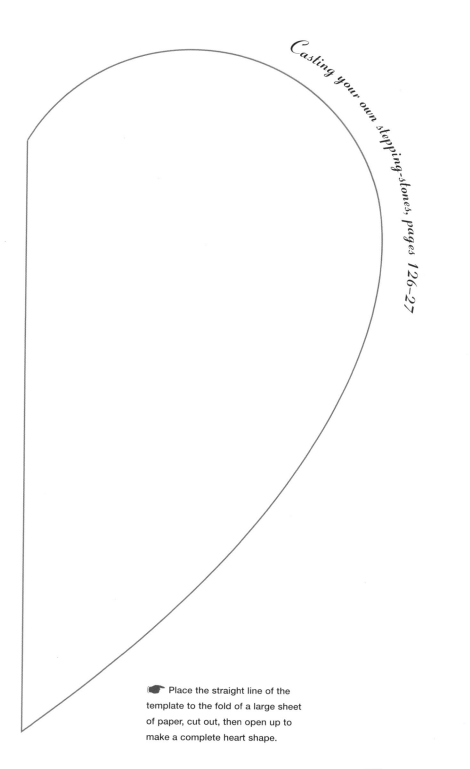

Casting your own stepping-stones, pages 126–27

☞ Place the straight line of the template to the fold of a large sheet of paper, cut out, then open up to make a complete heart shape.

☞ Mark eight eyelet positions with pencil crosses. Each one should be 1½ in. away from the fold lines and 4 in. in from the edge.

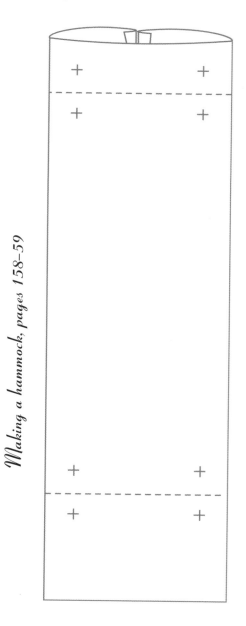

Making a hammock, pages 158–59

Making an art deco–style trellis, pages 152–53

☞ Cut all the pieces of wood to size as
indicated on page 153, then construct as
shown in the diagram below.

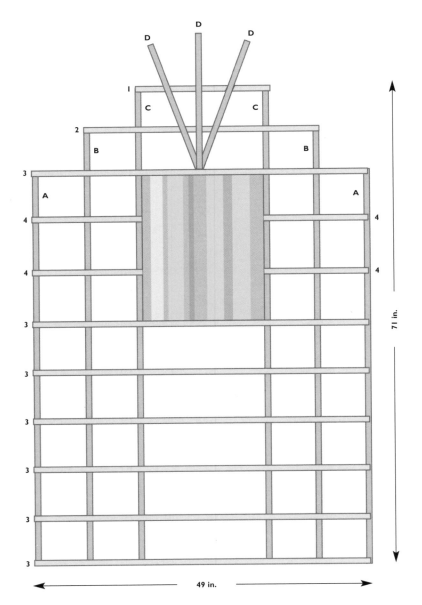

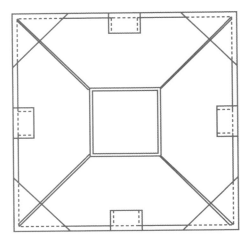

UNDERSIDE

Repairing a garden umbrella, pages 156–57

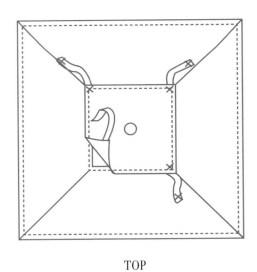

TOP

Building a barbecue, pages 164–65

☛ Build up the brick tower using the course diagrams as a guide. The structure will be quite sturdy and needs no mortar.

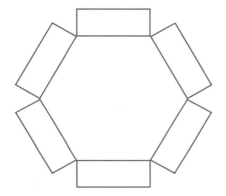

FIRST COURSE

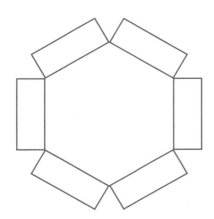

SECOND COURSE

Making a wood bin, pages 168–69

☛ Cut the rough-sawn wood pieces to the size indicated on page 169. Then simply drill screw holes and secure the wood bin together following the constructional diagram below.

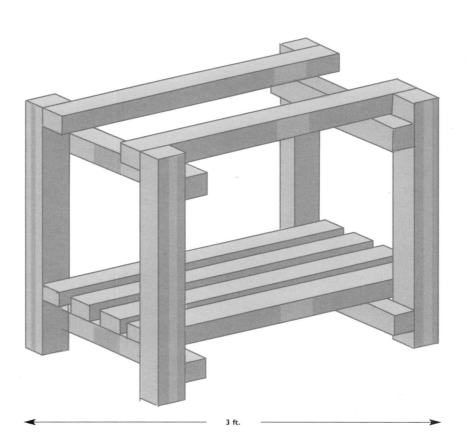

← 3 ft. →

185

GLOSSARY OF TERMS

AGGREGATES The term for materials (fine or coarse) that are added to a cement mix, such as sand, gravel, or larger stone lumps.

ALGAE Simple, nonflowering plants without roots, leaves, or stems, for example, seaweed, lichen, or moss.

ANGLE GRINDER An electrically powered tool with a heavy-duty revolving blade for cutting brick, metal, and stone.

ARMATURE The framework around which a structure is molded.

AUGER A long, flexible rod used to clear blockages from water and waste pipes.

AWL A small hand tool with a pointed spike, used to make pilot holes in wood.

BEVEL A slanting or sloping edge.

BEVEL SIDING BOARDS Wood boards that have one thick edge and one thin one, enabling them to be overlapped when used in fencing or construction.

BIB FAUCET An outdoor faucet.

BIT A metal attachment for a drill to facilitate drilling of holes of various diameter.

BRICK CHISEL A chisel with a wide blade for cutting bricks and pavers.

BUTT A joint between two pieces of wood. The pieces are cut square and one is butted to its neighbor. *Also:* Showcase body part that keeps its fine form with diligent home and yard maintenance.

BUTTERING The application of tile adhesive with a small knife.

CHALK LINE A tool that provides a straightedge *(see page 11)*.

CLEAT A narrow strip of wood or a T-shaped or similar projection that is used to secure a rope *(see page 100)*.

CLOSEBOARD FENCING Fencing made from overlapping bevel siding boards nailed onto horizontal wood rails.

COLD CHISEL A narrow chisel used in conjunction with a hammer to cut paving slabs, metal, etc.

CROSS-HALF-LAP JOINT A wood joint that makes use of slots cut into pieces of wood *(see page 167)*.

CROSS-HEAD The term for screws with a cross-shaped indentation in the head, for use with cross-head (Phillips) screwdrivers.

CROSS-RAIL A horizontal wood rail to which fence boards are attached.

DRAIN RODS Flexible rods that join together for use in clearing a blocked toilet.

DRY-LAYING Laying a patio or path without using mortar.

DUAL-PURPOSE LADDER A ladder that can be used as a stepladder or as an extension ladder.

EAVES The part of a roof that meets or overhangs the walls of a building.

EDGER An electrically powered tool for neatening lawn edges along paths or around irregular objects, such as trees.

EDGING TOOL A tool with a sharp, semicircular blade used for trimming the edge of a lawn.

EFFLORESCENCE A white powdery substance that forms on brick or mortar walls as a result of salts to migrating to the surface.

FINIAL A diamond-shaped piece of wood placed at the roof peak of a small building, or a decorative ornament at the top, end, or corner of an object.

FLASHING Metal strips (usually copper, aluminum, or galvanized steel) used to weatherproof the gaps between roofing surfaces. *Also:* The art of showing too much midriff in order to attract hunky contractor.

FLAT-HEAD The term for screws with a single slot-shaped indentation across the head. Also known as "slot-head."

FLUSH When two surfaces are perfectly level with each other. *Also:* Skin condition associated with getting a gorgeous contractor on the job (see STUD).

FOOTING A concrete support that is sunk into the ground and used to support a decking framework.

FORMWORK Temporary wood framework used as a guide and containment when laying a patio or path.

FRENCHMAN A hand tool used to scoop up excess mortar. *Also:* A charming language barrier worth having around the home and garden.

FROG A depression commonly found on one side of a brick that acts as a key for mortar. *Also:* Web-footed garden amphibian that can be kissed to reveal handsome prince.

GALVANIZED Covered with a protective layer of zinc. Objects manufactured from galvanized iron or steel are less prone to rust.

GFCI Ground fault circuit interrupter. A circuit-breaking safety device designed to provide protection from electric shock.

GLAZIER'S POINTS Small nails used to secure a glazed pane into a window frame.

GRAIN The direction or pattern of wood fibers.

GROUT Used to fill and seal the gaps between tiles after they have been attached to walls, and for other masonry repairs.

GUILLOTINE CUTTER A device for cutting paving slabs *(see page 16)*.

HASP AND STAPLE A device used in conjunction with a padlock to secure a door.

HEAVE The opposite of *SUBSIDENCE*. *Also*: Your least favorite verb, so take heed of protective clothing and equipment warnings when working with chemicals *(see page 69)*.

✳ I DIDN'T KNOW THAT WOOD BINS CAME IN A KIT!

JOIST A horizontal or metal supporting beam for walls, ceilings, or floors.

KEY The term referring to a surface that has been sanded ready for painting or gluing.

LADDER STAY A wood strip-and-peg device that enables you to secure a ladder in a safe position *(see page 19)*.

LAG SCREW These screws have a square head and are driven into the work using a wrench. Used for heavy-duty construction.

LANDSCAPE FABRIC Material used in external construction work. It allows water to drain downward to the earth beneath, but does not allow weeds or other organic material to penetrate upward.

LOPPER Giant pruners with long handles used for trimming trees and undergrowth.

MASKING TAPE Self-adhesive paper tape used to mask off areas when painting.

MITER Joint between two pieces of wood where the ends of each piece have been cut to the same angle.

MOISTURE-PROOF COURSE A layer of impervious material that is used to keep moisture from rising up into walls.

MORTAR Building material (a fine mixture of cement, lime, and sand) used to bond bricks and other masonry parts.

MULCH A mixture of leaves, bark, or compost material.

PAVER A paving brick.

PEGBOARD Perforated hardboard covered with predrilled holes.

PERGOLA An arched structure in a garden or yard that provides a framework for climbing or trailing plants.

PICKET A pointed, wooden stake used in certain types of fencing.

PIPE TAPE Pipe tape is used in plumbing to make watertight seals.

PILOT HOLE A preliminary hole drilled into sheet material to facilitate easy insertion of a jigsaw blade or small diameter hole used as guide for a screw.

PIR MOTION SENSOR PIR is an abbreviation for "passive infrared." PIR motion sensors are used in conjunction with outdoor safety lights; they detect movement within a given area, causing the lights to be switched on.

PLATE VIBRATOR An electrically powered flattening tool for use in landscaping projects *(see page 16)*.

POINTING The shaping of mortar joints between bricks *(see pages 70–71)*. *Also*: Hand action employed in order to show off successful outdoor projects to friends and family.

PLUGGING CHISEL A tool for removing loose mortar joints *(see page 14)*.

PLUMB LINE A device for finding true vertical lines *(see page 15)*.

PRESSURE-TREATED LUMBER Wood for outdoor use that has been specially treated with preservatives.

PUTTY KNIFE A knife for applying and shaping filler *(see page 14)*.

RABBET A rectangular recess found along the edge of a frame or molded workpiece.

RISER The vertical portion of a step.

RISING MAIN The name given to the first section of water pipe in a domestic plumbing system. It usually enters the house under the kitchen sink and follows the wall upward.

SHIM Wedge-shaped pieces of wood used as supports.

* WHAT DO YOU MEAN ALISON JENKINS TELLS IT BETTER THAN I DO?

SHUTOFF VALVE A faucet with a valve and a washer that is inserted into the main water pipe in order to control water flow.

SIDING Interlocking or overlapping boards made of vinyl, aluminum, or wood that cover the exterior walls of a building.

SLEDGEHAMMER A heavy hammer for use in cutting paving slabs, or other heavy work.

SOLEPLATES Wood lengths laid on concrete footings across a decking site that support the joists and deck construction.

SPIGOT A device for controlling the flow of liquid in a faucet.

SPINDLE The rod or pin around which a door handle revolves.

SPLINING TOOL A screen-installation tool (see page 82).

STEEL WOOL Fine metal fibers gathered together to form a pad used for sanding.

STRAINING WIRE/WINDING BRACKET Mechanism used to keep the mesh of a wire fence taut and secure.

STRINGER A shaped side panel that supports stair treads. *Also*: Subcontractor who can save your life on the more complicated jobs.

STUD Vertical lumber which forms part of a wallboard partition wall. *Also*: More abundant in the path of us do-it-yourselfers, found in key supply stops, such as Home Depot and the like. Worth the work!

SUBSIDENCE The gradual caving in or sinking of an area of ground.

TAMPING A method for leveling and compacting loose earth or other substances (see page 117).

THRESHOLD A piece of wood attached permanently across the entrance to a door. *Also*: Prime entryways over which truly romantic STUDS carry us hard-working girls at the end of a hard day's work.

TINE A prong or sharp point, such as on a garden fork.

TIN SNIPS A tool for cutting metal and vinyl materials. Particularly useful for roofing jobs (see page 14).

TREAD The horizontal part of a step.

TRELLIS An ornamental latticework frame used as a support for climbing plants or dividing screen in a garden.

TRY SQUARE A tool used as a guide to mark square corners (see page 15). *Also*: At times, far more reliable than the STUD or that stunning FRENCHMAN.

VOLATILE ORGANIC COMPOUND A chemical compound that participates in photochemical reactions. Such compounds are associated with poor air quality and the production of carcinogens.

WALL ANCHOR Plastic sleeve to fit a screw. The wall anchor is inserted into a predrilled hole in a wall. When the screw is inserted, it then expands to form a firm gripping surface for the screw's head.

WASHER Rubber disk found in a faucet.

WEATHER-SEAL MOLDING A molded strip of wood attached across the bottom of an inward-opening external door.

FURTHER READING

Other titles by Laurel Glen include:

100 THINGS YOU DON'T NEED A MAN FOR!—HOME REPAIR AND IMPROVEMENT

Alison Jenkins

1-57145-537-X

ANNIE SLOAN'S COLOR SCHEMES

Annie Sloan

1-57145-761-5

CREATING GARDEN PONDS AND WATER FEATURES

Debbie Roberts and Ian Smith

1-57145-492-6

GARDEN LIGHTING

John Raine

1-57145-692-9

Coming in January 2003:

GARDEN BOUNDARIES

Toby Buckland

1-57145-823-9

GARDEN SURFACES

Richard Key

1-57145-824-7

SUPPLIERS

ACE HARDWARE

2200 Kensington Ct.

Oak Brook, IL 60523-2100

(630) 990-6600

www.acehardware.com

FORK & SPADE

1313 Scenic Drive

Modesto, CA 95355

(800) 829-5919

www.forkandspade.com

GARDENER'S SUPPLY COMPANY

128 Intervale Road

Burlington, VT 05401

(888) 833-1412

www.gardeners.com

HOME DEPOT

2455 Pace Ferry Rd.

Atlanta, GA 30339

(800) 430-3376

www.homedepot.com

IKEA

www.ikea.com

LOWE'S HOME IMPROVEMENT WAREHOUSE

P.O. Box 1111

North Wilkesboro, NC 28656

(800) 44-LOWES

www.lowes.com

PLOW & HEARTH

(800) 494-7544

www.plowhearth.com

RESTORATION HARDWARE

15 Koch Road, Suite J

Corte Madera, CA 94925-1240

(800) 816-0969

www.restorationhardware.com

ROGER'S GARDENS

2301 San Joaquin Hills Road

Corona Del Mar, CA 92625

(800) 647-2356

www.rogersgardens.com

SEEDS OF CHANGE

(888) 762-7333

www.seedsofchange.com

SMITH & HAWKEN

(800) 940-1170

www.smithandhawken.com

TARGET

(888) 304-4000

www.target.com

TRUE VALUE HARDWARE

8600 W. Bryn Mawr Avenue

Chicago, IL 60631-3505

(773) 695-5000

www.truevalue.com

Index

✳ DON'T MIND
ME, I'M NOT EVEN
IN THE INDEX!

Acknowledgments

AUTHOR ACKNOWLEDGMENTS

I'd like to dedicate this book to my Mam and Dad, Adrian, Daisy and William, M&M, Helen, David and Keryl, and all the other lovely people I am so lucky to have as friends and family. Thanks to Caroline for support, services rendered, and loan of nodding cat. Many, many thanks to Clare for bed & breakfast, girlie solidarity, and positive reinforcement! Last but not least, a great big thank you to all at The Ivy Press and the studio for all the hard work, perseverance, and encouragement—we got there in the end!

PICTURE CREDITS

Corbis Images Joseph Sohm 77br, Lee Snider 82m, Macduff Everton 82mr, Michael Boys 162bl & 162bm
Getty Images Mike Kelly 87bl
Homelec 36br, 163ml, 163m, 163mr, 163tr
Hozelock Cyprio (www.hozelock.com) 37bl & 37bm, 173m & 173tr
Micromark 150br, 151bl, & 151br

☞ The author and publisher would like to thank the following for their assistance and for the loan of props:
Black and Decker (all power tools)
Bluebell, Brighton
Cissy Mo, Brighton
Focus Do-It All (garden shed)
HSS Hire shops (rental equipment)
International Paints (floor paint, vinyl paint, metal paint)
Jaymart (artificial grass)
Harris (paintbrushes)
Hozelock (water feature hose and attachments, garden lights)
Kitschen Sync., London
Ronseal (wood stains and decking sealants and treatments)
Toolbank (hand tools, toolbelt, toolbox)
South Coast Roofing Supplies (roof tiles)
Stanley (hand tools)

✳ I'D LIKE TO THANK MY AGENT, MY STYLIST, MY HAIR GURU, MY SCRIPT EDITOR, MY NAIL ARTIST, MY MOM, MY DOG, MY CAT...